ALLEN COUNTY PUBLIC LIBRARY

D1448112

INVITE

Preaching for Response

O. DEAN MARTIN

DISCIPLESHIP RESOURCES
MATERIALS FOR GROWTH IN CHRISTIAN FAITH AND LIFE

P.O. Box 189 • Nashville, TN 37202 • Phone (615) 340-7285

JUL 2 6 2003

PATHWAYS TO CHURCH GROWTH SERIES

Taking Attendance: Growing Through Worship, Hoyt L. Hickman

The First Year: Incorporating New Members, Suzanne G. Braden

Invite: Preaching for Response, O. Dean Martin

Library of Congress Catalog Card No.: 87-71062

ISBN 0-88177-044-2

INVITE: PREACHING FOR RESPONSE. Copyright © 1987 by O. Dean Martin. All rights reserved. Printed in the United States of America. No part of this book may be reproduced in any manner whatsoever without written permission except in the case of brief quotations embodied in critical articles or reviews. For information address Discipleship Resources Editorial Offices, P. O. Box 840, Nashville, Tennessee 37202.

DR044B

DEDICATION

This book is dedicated to my son, The Reverend James Thomas Martin, just beginning his "ministry of invitation."

This book is also dedicated to the pastor who understands that inherent in the gospel is an invitation to respond to the gospel. To the local pastor who gives people the opportunity to respond to this gospel but does so in a logical, nonmanipulative, and sensitive way. To the servant of the congregation who deeply appreciates the words of St. Paul to the Church at Corinth (2 Cor. 4:1,2, The Living Bible), "It is God himself, in his mercy, who has given us this wonderful work, and so we never give up. We do not try to trick people into believing—we are not interested in fooling anyone. . . . All such shameful methods we forego." But, having foregone such shameful methods, this book is dedicated to the pastor who still seeks meaningful, courteous, and deliberate ways of inviting response to the proclamation of the hour.

CONTENTS

FOREWORD

United Methodist churches throughout the world are making covenants to grow in ministry and grow in numbers. We believe that church growth will come as a result of our witness and service in the world. We know that churches grow when Christians share their faith stories with persons who are alienated from God and not involved in the life of the church. We gain this perspective from reading scripture, from studying the conversion experiences of Christians through the centuries, and from our own personal experience.

We also know that as disciples we must receive new persons in our congregations and avoid judging their faith stories or dismissing their struggle to know God. Thus we help all persons relate to God and develop Christian faith, equipping them and sending them out as disciples of the one who is the Lord of all life.

We can translate this evangelistic commission into the language of those who study the reasons for church growth. One fruitful way to describe the reasons for church growth is to identify 1) factors that attract persons to the gospel and the church, 2) factors that influence persons to make a commitment to Christ and membership in a congregation, and 3) factors that bond persons in their relationship with Christ and the church.

Each pastor and each lay minister of the gospel knows that there are no snappy solutions, no easy five or ten steps which should result in "x" number of persons attending Sunday morning worship. Yet we can identify factors that focus our prayer and ministry on the pathways to church growth. Pastors of growing churches prefer to rank the factors which contribute to membership growth. Our research shows that the top ten factors are:

1. Vital worship services
2. Fellowship and relational settings
3. Pastor and pastoral functions
4. Sharply targeted ministries
5. Community/world outreach
6. Christian education
7. Growth posture/planning
8. Physical facilities and location
9. Lay leadership/involvement
10. Evangelism activities

This series, Pathways to Church Growth, includes books and booklets containing practical suggestions for ministry related to these ten factors. The resources are written by leaders in the church and by successful pastors of growing churches. This book by O. Dean Martin urges decisive preaching which issues invitations and requires response for commitment of many kinds to Jesus Christ. Dean gives several models to show how to conclude the sermon effectively as you intentionally invite the congregation to make knowledgeable commitment.

I invite you to join together with Christians everywhere in redoubling your ministry and commitment to a growing church. Tell your story about what God has done for you, and encourage people in your community who want to know how Christ makes a difference in our lives.

EZRA EARL JONES
General Secretary
General Board of Discipleship
The United Methodist Church

INTRODUCTION

This enlarged and rewritten book appeared in 1970. This second expanded incarnation is in response to requests from the General Board of Discipleship of The United Methodist Church as well as from ministers across the country. In this day and time, when The United Methodist Church is a rapidly declining denomination many people are saying; if our gospel is right, if our spirit is right, if our heritage is honorable, and if our compassion is undiminished, what is the problem?

We cannot say the problem identified in this book is *the* problem, but we can say that a conspicuous lack of decisiveness is certainly one of the problems. At least one of our fatal but correctable flaws is a general unwillingness to extend meaningful evangelistic invitations.

I advocate being decisive, or being invitational, as an important starting point for further renewal of our church, and that is precisely what this book is all about! What is *invitation*? How can a church in general, or a minister specifically, of any denomination be more decisive? Regardless of affiliation, what does the preacher do with the conclusion of the service when he or she wants to be decisive but not manipulative, authentic but not autocratic?

The perspectives shared in this work grow out of my own frustrations as a pastor and as a church bureaucrat. For years, as a pastor, I struggled with the problem of decisiveness, the invitation following the sermon. Then, for three years it was my privilege to serve on the staff of The General Board of Discipleship of The United Methodist Church. As a minister in the section on Field Service, I traveled extensively throughout the United States. Again and again I was struck with the dilemma and the nondeliberateness surrounding the "evangelistic invitation," particularly as that subject applies to the Sunday morning worship service. I found many people, including myself, not at all unlike the minister in Iowa who turned to me one Sunday and said, "What do you do when you've finished the sermon?"

Like me, most of the pastors I worked with knew something about being decisive, that is, about extending an invitation in a revival or missional setting. We fathom something of the mechanics or methodology of encouraging response at youth retreats. And, we certainly have catalogued adequate data on how to ignore or circumvent decisive evangelism. But, we have been granted precious little information on how to extend an invitation at the all-important, inordinately strategic morning worship service! Little attempt has been made to systematize the few guidelines and bits of information that are available. Seminaries (with rare exceptions) tend not to touch the important subject of invitation with a ten foot shepherd's crook. Instead, they safely concentrate on turning out ministers who are "intellectually sound" and "relevant." At best, these "relevant" ministers tend to be people who know a great deal about presenting their product but precious little about giving people a chance to *buy* the product! They lack decisiveness.

Following a general and fundamentally indecisive academic indoctrination, the local pastor then goes to his or her first charge and finds parishioners saying either "you're going to burn in hell if you don't start giving altar calls" or "please don't drag us back into old-fashioned revivalism!" The net result, in many of today's pulpits, is a sad array of ambivalence, ambiguity, and an ever-broadening sense of incompleteness and frustration.

Then, as a final, almost lethal blow, if anyone at all endeavors to pass along information, the pastor is dogmatically informed that he or she really has only two basic options. The pastor must either give an old-fashioned "altar call" (singing fifty verses of "Just as I Am") or offer up a cold, calculatedly ambiguous phrase called something like "An Invitation to Christian Discipleship" which, translated, means either "Won't you please come join the church" or "I wish I knew what I was doing, and I hope this little phrase somehow covers for me!"

Some time ago a district superintendent expressed our dilemma in the following way. He recounted one of the most frustrating situations of his entire ministry. "I was preaching the other Sunday morning in one of the churches in my district," he said, "and God was really evident in the service. You could simply feel the Holy Spirit working! I came to the end of the service. I was confused and bewildered. I simply did not know how to close the service! I finally announced a hymn, and we all left feeling incomplete and frustrated. As my wife and I got into the car to drive away, she said, 'Why didn't you give some kind of invitation!' I lamely responded, "I know I was supposed to do something, but as I looked about the congregation I knew everyone there was either a member of the church or had already become a Christian. I simply did not know what to do!"

There are other options. The invitation, when understood as inherent to the gospel, is a great deal more than either institutional recruitment or an anachronism from the sawdust trail.

The invitation at the close of the service is the *many-faceted* opportunity for people.to say "yes," or "no," or "wait" to the message of the hour. **Any message worth preaching requires an opportunity for invitation!** Any congregation hearing the proclamation of a gospel worth hearing expects such an opportunity!

Our quest at this point is simple: A person preaches either for *response* or for *display*! Whenever we as pastors approach the pulpit for the period of proclamation, we are basically and simply pursuing one of two courses: We are asking people to think we are wonderful (and if they have responded at that point then there is no further response necessary), or, we are asking them (right now!) to deal with the issue before us in some logical sequence of commitment.

This book is an attempt to present some of the helpful insights shared with me by creative and sensitive pastors across America as well as ministers with whom I have worked in other countries. These men and women have clearly chosen the best option: to preach for response! This book is from them and for them.

1. THE INSTITUTION

The ability to be decisive in evangelism and preaching is very much bound up in a larger question—can I function in this environment, this institution?

During my first year on the staff of the General Board of Evangelism of The United Methodist Church I was sent on assignment to Wilmington, Delaware. About twelve of us on the general staff were doing inner-city work at a coffeehouse in downtown Wilmington. When the weekend arrived, each of us was given a preaching assignment for Sunday morning. My assignment was a large, high church Episcopal congregation just a few blocks from our headquarters (the YMCA). When I arrived at the church, I discovered the morning service lasted an hour and a half, but only ten minutes of that time was set aside for the sermon. I negotiated with the senior minister to gain more preaching time by assisting him with the Eucharist. Without this adjustment, I was unable to do my ministry, be decisive, or in any way adequately function within this institutional setting. The setting, the environment, and the institution constitute a primary consideration!

It is for the reason of setting that some preachers leave the local church. They imply "I cannot be a decisive proclaimer in this institution!" They may appropriately turn instead to the military as a chaplain, to a local hospital, to working under a large tent, or to freewheeling it on a street corner. My choice has been the congregation. And, the institution, the *container* of my ministry, is as important to further reflection as is the time I climbed up on a diving board to sail off into a big swimming pool, only to discover, in the nick of time, that the pool was empty. It had been drained of all its water! The local church is my container. It is the pool of my choice, and I want to know if I can swim in this environment.

The institutional church has come under severe fire in our day, and justly so! Soren Kiekegaard was right when he said, "The church is a whore but she is my mother." It is an institution that is made up of imperfect people talking about perfection, stumbling people speaking of walking upright, fragile people speaking of eternal things. It has prostituted itself, promised, procrastinated, and puttered about until, as someone has said, "Perhaps the greatest proof of the existence of God is that he has survived the church." But then we look around and find God working through the

1

church, through all its imperfections, thorns, and blemishes to give *life* to people, places, and things! It may have its problems, but it has been the instrument of new birth for so many.

So, we decide, "Yes! I can dive into this pool! There is water enough for me to swim!" Then, once in, we often find things floating around in the water itself that make swimming difficult. We become like the young man who left my church to enter seminary to follow his call into the ministry. After three years in seminary and about two years in his first appointment, his comment to me was, "I've discovered there is a world of difference between *religious* work and *church* work."

In the church pool there are often sharks of subtle breed and description. There are also schools of miscellaneous piranha; there are deep ruts and petrified preconceptions that are anything but subtle. We quickly discover "committee" attitudes boldly proclaiming that the Holy Spirit cannot work unless one files "in triplicate" with the home office for assistance; that a "kit" for every catastrophe awaits one's order at headquarters. And, there's always the parochial congregational attitude that says, "We've always stood on this corner and therefore we shall forever stand." Or, the most lethal cry of them all, "We've never done it that way before!" All these, and more, are part of the setting, the swimming pool, the institution. Can we work there? Is it possible to be decisive and effective within this framework? The simple answer is that most people who are decisive can be decisive anywhere. Though simplistic, I think this statement is fundamentally accurate. But I think we need to move beyond the simple answer and raise the question to a more complex level. What if I want to stop jumping from one institution to another, always and forever starting over? What if I really would like to swim in the local church. How can I come to terms with my chosen institution?

The answer here is the same answer we find elsewhere in life. Choose the mate you want for life and then, rather than continually blaming the choice, work on the personal problems you have that would make any choice unacceptable! Or, as someone has pointed out, "Wherever you go, there you are." So, if you like this marriage, it will work if you work on yourself and it. Keep on keeping on! If you are a pastor to the congregation and feel God wants you to be in the local church, fix it by fixing yourself and going on from there to bigger and better things! Gypsy Smith, a famous evangelist of an earlier day, once said, "The way to experience renewal is to get by yourself in a room. Draw a circle in the floor around you and then ask God to change everything inside that circle."

This is not to claim that the institution of my choice is in need of no fixing, but "wherever I go, there I am." And until I work on myself I add but more imperfection to any imperfect institution I may choose for my life's work!

In my own mind I have come to see the problem in quite another way than that of the well-worn paths of blaming the inanimate "thing." The problem many of us are experiencing across this land today is not so much an "institutional dilemma" as much as it is a problem of personality conflict. Much of our struggle with institutionalism, as bad as some institutions can be, is in reality a personal maturity/immaturity forum disguised to protect our *individual* psyche! Until this possibility is explored, and brought into practical experience, many of our current frustrations, anguish, and bitterness will remain in the arena of symptoms, and consequently remain unresolved. In other words, scapegoats will remain in high demand. Not only will *we* remain unfixed but the scapegoat also remains unfixed.

We must move from the obvious faults and imperfections of our church and deal forthrightly with the immaturities within ourselves that (1) prevent us from serving within our chosen structure, and (2) negate our effectiveness in renewing our chosen structure!

This kind of dual cure can be applied in these words once we realize that all activities institutionalize, and in all institutionalizing there is a personal maturation ceiling which must be pushed through in order to continue personal growth (maturing). By changing the institutions one does not compensate or facilitate!

Love is a good example. Love is an activity that, to survive, must become institutionalized (marriage). Just going steady, or living together, or being eternally devoted is not a strong enough container. Consequently, many of today's consenting roommates are finding their love oozing out through the porous container of *quasi*-institutionalization. So, for those of us who want to keep our love, and see our love mature, marriage offers a safer container. We get married! We institutionalize our inspiration!

Anyone who has been married for over fifteen minutes already knows there comes a time (and times) when the relationship isn't honeymoon but, for that moment, is pure homework. I call that sporadic but predictable increment the "Maturation Ceiling." The M.C. is that point to which the marriage (he and she, the church and me, my job and me, etc.) grows easily but now has risen to a barrier (a ceiling) that demands greater maturation on my part for me to break out into a higher floor of the relationship. Some of us bump our heads on these periodic ceilings. We find problems in the relationship, sharks in the pond, problems with the arrangements, and we start thinking divorce. "Let me out of this so I can find a marriage that requires nothing of me!" We cry, "Give me something that is easy and never comes along asking for maturity as the price of further expanding the relationship!" Then, we remarry, only to discover that by changing institutions we do not compensate or facilitate. We discover, eventually, that if we leave the current institution *because we do not want to grow up*, we go out but to face the same set of circumstances in our next marriages, only sooner and with more intensity! With our frenetic hopping about, we become like the man who entered my office one time and said, "Pastor, I'm not a member of your congregation but I want to get married and want you to perform the ceremony." I knew the man only by reputation. I said, "Haven't you been married before?" "Yes," he answered, "seven times." I then asked, "Have you learned anything yet?" "Yes," he replied honestly, "I've finally learned that I'm carrying most of the problems around inside me."

That's no way to live! We need to deal with ourselves and Maturation Ceilings that will come in any relationship. Again by staying with the analogy of marriage to illustrate the broader principle, I often follow this approach in the typical counseling situation. A man enters my office and says, "Dean, I'm divorcing my wife and marrying my secretary, and I wanted you to hear it from me first!" I respond by saying, "I can certainly understand that! I've seen your secretary, and she's a real knockout. Besides that, your wife is as old as you are, and we both know how unacceptable that is! However, as your friend and as someone who really cares about you, allow me to make just one practical suggestion. Do not divorce your wife until you have made your present marriage a beautiful, fantastic relationship. When you have accomplished this, you may then consider divorce without crippling your own maturation process. For, if you do not break through 'the ceiling' that is irritating you in your present marriage, you'll probably not do it in the next; and, if you do make a beautiful marriage out of what you've got, you may want to keep on with it. Just think of the alimony you'll save!"

As a reminder, and as a source of encouragement, we see this principle of "hanging in, breaking through, and moving on up" in virtually every conceivable commitment of life. For instance, a few blocks from where I once lived while serving an inner-city church in Miami, there existed a subculture group. The *Miami Herald* carried an interesting series of articles on this group as they "left" our society and climbed up into the sprawling branches of a large tropical banyan tree to "create a new and better society." As the series documented, it was not long before about half the original group had climbed down out of that tree to go up another tree to establish yet another "perfect" society (having met, again, the same frustrations encountered in the original version). Finally, someone noticed a lot of kids sitting in banyan trees throughout the area, each one "copping out" at precisely the same maturation ceiling that instigated their climbing up the initial tree in the first place.

Let us remain ever grateful for citizens who stay on the ground, do not accept the status quo, but hang in there. They break through the ceiling of personal frustration and actually help themselves and their society.

Dr. J. Wallace Hamilton, one of America's great preachers of the twentieth century, once applied this same principle to sermon preparation. He said many pastors never improve in their sermon preparation, or delivery, because there comes a point in the preparation of a sermon where it is so hard to keep digging, struggling, and perfecting. We have our three points and a poem, and that is where we customarily assume completion of the task. Upon acquiring this infallible format, we move quickly to accept the task as finished so as to avoid the descending birth pangs of greater clarity, inspiration, and direction. In many marriages, in dealing with society, in sermon preparation, we stop at the "ceiling" and never fathom the joy and fulfillment of going on and going up beyond mediocrity! What if I want to stop jumping from one institution to another, always and forever starting over? What if I really would like to swim in the local church? How can I come to terms with my chosen institution? Begin by saying, "I want to pastor a congregation! God has called me to this job, and I dare to believe I can have a decisive ministry within this framework!" Then, don't be hesitant at all to recognize the fact that this chosen institution needs vast improvement, updating, and renewal! Be attuned to the reality that constructive, loving, *insider* criticism is healthy for any organization.

I once knew a man who was appointed to a church that was "dead." The new minister had a lot of buildings, in a strategic location, and a few people to help, but the congregation itself was not "alive" and "relevant." My friend proceeded to leave this appointment *and* his denomination by beginning his own church, which would be what a real church ought to be! So, he went out, bought land, got a few people to help, and finally built a building. He did all this to get back to where he could have started. He could have been, as many are, the pastor who stayed with what he had, dealt with the place where he always wanted to stop, back off, and run. This approach would have saved an awful lot of alimony.

The greatest opportunity to help renew and involve the institutional church is in the morning worship hour! I believe that if *whatever* needs to transpire within a particular congregation does not happen in the morning service, it probably isn't going to happen! This personal prejudice keeps our sights on the specific subject of the moment—inviting. Sunday morning is when we need to learn to be decisive, to be invitational.

2. UNDERSTANDING CHURCH GROWTH

Unless we explore the real meaning and means of church growth, someone may falsely conclude that any talk about being "decisive" and "invitational" is simply due to the fact that a number of mainline churches are facing drastic membership decline. This is certainly the correlation many United Methodists have in mind today when we hear such things as, "The United Methodist Church must become a more evangelistic church!" "We must become a church that reaches people for Christ!" "We must get our zeal back" and so on.

One quickly discovers what some people are fearfully saying: Let's reverse membership loss. Let's get to work so we can hold our heads up again. Let's extend "evangelistic invitations" *because* we need more members to survive.

If you doubt this assessment, ask yourself how often you recall hearing the phrase "we must become more evangelistic" *before* our membership graft began dropping like a lead balloon! At most, there was a voice here and a voice there, crying in the wilderness.

So, when we speak of extending the evangelistic invitation (*evangelistic* and *invitation* defined in Chapter 4), and do so in a period of membership decline and mixed motivations, let us be clear about the nature of church growth.

As By-Product

First we must understand church growth, not as getting more members, but as the logical by-product of being a church worth joining. We should see that growth is not the goal but that relevant Good News is the goal. Increased membership follows as a result; that if preachers (and any other group, for that matter) will preach a practical gospel worth responding to, and actually extend a clear invitation to respond, nobody will have to concentrate on church growth.

Churches will pursue one of two alternatives: be a church worth joining or, lacking that, learn how to make people join even if the experience is meaningless to their personal lives. The second alternative focuses on getting more members.

6

As D. Elton Trueblood once observed, the primary reason for the decline of mainline Christianity is that it is dull. People want help. Everyone is reaching out for security, encouragement, practical assistance, challenge, and meaningful involvement. The churches that are growing are ministering to these needs because such churches are worth joining.

Put another way, if people are not joining a church it is either because there is something wrong with their faith or there is something wrong with the church soliciting their involvement. Therefore, the "invitation" is not to join a church, or buttress up a flagging institution. Church growth is about being the kind of church worth joining so that people who have a faith that needs fixing will have somewhere to go to get it fixed. Saving the institution is never the point.

Jesus gave us significant forewarning that "whoever attempts to save his life will lose it but whoever loses his life for my sake will find it." Church growth is about the business of growing because people are being invited to give their lives to Christ and share his concern for the world. These are the churches that are growing, the ones that are trying not to save themselves but salvage as much of the world as can possibly be salvaged.

A professor once visited my office. He was a member of the faculty of The University of Florida, just down the street from the church, and he was transferring to a new faculty position at another university. He was a new Christian with minimal background in faith and most anxious to find a new fellowship that would help him keep his faith and continue to grow in his life. His question to me was, "Is there a church of our denomination where I am moving?" I said, "Certainly! We've got thousands of churches all over the country." "Really?" he said rather incredulously, "I don't know much about churches, as you know, but I've never noticed an 'Exciting United Methodist Church' anywhere in my life!" I had no idea why he was talking this way and asked for further enlightenment. Finally he called my attention to one of our blue shield road signs down on the corner and said, "That church! That denomination!" Then, realizing his very minimal religious background, I finally understood.

When I first came to Trinity United Methodist Church in Gainesville, Florida, we were surrounded by four major intersections and had no church signs anywhere. Most people didn't even know Trinity existed. I ordered eight new signs, two for each intersection, but did not waste time with printing that said "Two Blocks," "Welcome Three Blocks," etc. I simply had a large arrow printed at the bottom of each sign pointing in the direction of Trinity Church. Above each arrow I had printed one word representing our goals for ourselves as a fellowship. This meant that at each intersection there was a different adjective describing what we were determined to be. I figured people would read such words over and over again. A sign that says "Two Blocks" runs out of inspiration pretty quickly! Our selected adjectives (goals) for the four intersections were: "Alive," "Involved," "Caring," and "Exciting." My friend lived near the sign which said *Exciting*, and, knowing no more than he did about churches or denominations, he had assumed that was the name of the denomination. And, he wanted to find another "Exciting United Methodist Church!"

The first thing we need to understand about church growth is that we should not push for new members. We should give every ounce of strength, vision, and commitment to being a church of Jesus Christ worth joining!

As Legitimate Choice

Second, while everybody needs a church, not everybody needs any church! People have different needs, hopes, dreams, tastes in liturgy and understandings of both worship and gospel (what, in fact, at this time in their lives is Good News for them). They will be making legitimate choices of what they consider to be churches worth joining based on those present needs.

This being true, growing churches or denominations are actually meeting a real or imagined personal need. This growing church does not even attempt to "be all things to all people and nothing to nobody." Instead, it zeroes in on its specific message for its specific world.

For instance, the latest research data on church growth show that growing churches tend to be loving churches. That is, congregations whose members possess an experience in Christ that fosters and promotes a loving environment are seeing church growth as a result of that environment. In fact, a loving environment is so essential to church growth that all of us know churches that work on *contrived* love, often called "love bombing." This contrived love is superficial, manipulative, and pragmatic. But it serves to fortify the premise that love, real or contrived, is so essential to church growth that, if such an atmosphere does not come via legitimately changed hearts and minds, then your group will likely learn to fake it! Faking it is not recommended. Possessing it, or rather being possessed by it, is far more commendable. People seek out a congregation that meets real needs, and perhaps one of the greatest needs of our day is the need to feel loved.

It is no wonder people are flocking to "loving" churches, contrived *or* authentic. Many of us are like the little boy who was left on the pediatrics floor of All Saints Hospital in Salt Lake City, Utah. His nurse hurried down to the office for a minute, turned on the intercom in his room to monitor his well-being by listening to his play, heard nothing, and finally said, "Billy! Billy!! Say something, Billy, I know you are in there!" Finally, after a long and frightening few moments little Billy said, "What do you want, wall?"

Like little Billy, most of us prefer warm, loving presence! We are tired of sterile, proper, staid, sanctified, and petrified assemblies. The church growth experts rightly observe that the loving congregations are seeing the most growth, but this is but an expression, a symptom, of the basic premise that people join churches that meet specific, immediate, and real needs!

The need to be loved, feel accepted, discern warmth and appreciation is but one expression of specific needs aching to be met. Others are just as hungry for a church actively involved in its community and world. Still others are seeking a message of positive possibility, or help in healing. Perhaps their need is for a message of prophetic judgment. Whatever their message, churches must concentrate on legitimate messages from God that meet real human needs.

The movie industry understands this principle of zeroing in on a specific group or need. They make little serious attempt to produce a movie that will "appeal to everyone." Instead, precisely because they want their theaters full, they concentrate on movies that appeal to teenagers, kung fu lovers, or romantics. The music industry does not attempt to put out a sheet of music that will appeal to everyone. Rather, various companies will concentrate on opera, operettas, light opera, Grand Ole Opry, rock and roll, hard rock, religious music, standard romantic, or perhaps country and western. Whenever they publish, they select a special segment of society to target.

Allow a brief restatement of my fundamental premise. I am not saying that you find a message which will appeal to someone who will fill your church and help make its budget. I am saying, however, that you and I, as preachers of the gospel, have a message that is uniquely God's and special to us. If we preach that message—God's message as we have been enlightened—there are many people hungering for just that message! On the other hand, if we try to give them everything, if we continue to offer up some nebulous "invitation to Christian discipleship," we will continue to address predominantly empty pews. We must, prayerfully and faithfully, discern and affirm our special message from God and lovingly and *deliberately* share that message (or tone, or accent, or emphasis) with our world.

Norman Vincent Peale presented his message with inordinate integrity. E. Stanley Jones did the very same thing with his message of evangelism and within the framework of intellectual respectability. *Time* magazine (Spring 1986) pointed out that, in their opinion, Jimmy Swaggart has concentrated his ministry on fear, Robert Schuller on peace, and Oral Roberts on health. Each of us, like each of these men, may adequately and meaningfully cover other or all aspects of the gospel. Our preaching, our personal message accent may be fear, or personal peace and prosperity, or health, or missions, or social concerns, or any of a number of affinities or preoccupations. We are all different, and each of us has a very special message from God. Share it gladly and decisively, and someone will hear it gladly.

Not long ago two friends, both members of an American Baptist church in another state, were discussing the hypothetical question of what would happen to their church if I, O. Dean Martin, were to come as their pastor. After a moment of reflection one friend said, "The church would be half empty by the middle of the first year. Then, we would have to tear the building down and build one twice as large!"

He was simply saying that many of the folks who presently attended that church legitimately did not need my personal message from God, or did not think they needed it, or just plain wouldn't accept it. But, once the new message of the new messenger was established, there would be, in their opinion, many others who would respond eagerly!

I think we must begin understanding this fundamental premise of communication. If The United Methodist Church, or any church, is to grow again, it must take seriously what the book publishers, the movie makers, and the song writers already know. Be specific! Have a message that is authentically yours, that comes genuinely from God through you, and share it with deliberateness and decisiveness. You may and should center that message around the church year, the lectionary, or some other vehicle promoting a full review of the gospel story, but it must be your special and specific message.

While sharing your special message throughout the cycle of years (be it hope, tolerance, healing, social concern, personal conversion, etc.)— you will, in the course of the years, touch on everything you know and feel about the gospel in general, but that message must retain its specific

3 1833 04430 0041

integrity. If you do that, the people who can and will respond to your specific message, will hear you gladly.

I've often stated the same premise in various pastor's schools and retreats. Churches that are full and growing are not full because they "preach the gospel" (as smug fundamentalism asserts) but because they meet needs. We who are United Methodists are often and unnecessarily cowed by the accusation that we are in decline because we do not "preach the gospel." Not true! In my travels all over this country, over and over again I've seen churches packed to the rafters that preach little more than a mixture of Old Testament gloom and doom coupled with promises of riches here and in the hereafter for blind compliance. There is not a touch of the gospel anywhere in sight. I have also seen churches where a loving Good News of God was shared regularly but in a very general way void of invitational decisiveness and, despite the gospel message, remained mostly empty. Gospel is not what *fills* churches. One may preach the gospel, say all the right words, without any relevancy, and people will not come. Meeting needs, scratching where somebody itches, is what fills churches and as a by-product causes churches to grow.

Some of these "needs" are legitimate, and some needs are but souls collecting preachers who will say what their itching ears long to hear. I know this danger of relativity, but I also know that I, prayerfully and carefully, can give my very special message, give it intently and decisively, and people will respond.

Remember that people tend to join churches in direct relationship to (1) their personal mental health and (2) individual emotional stability. Let's look briefly at these needs.

Simply if not simplistically stated, some people need a church where they are told exactly what to think and precisely how to act. You and I may counter by saying, "If that's the way they are, then that kind of church is exactly what they do not need." True! But, people have to start from where they are or they aren't going anywhere. Consequently, some people emotionally need a church with a Big Daddy. You and I, who do not operate as "Big Daddies" need not feel badly because they choose such a church. There are plenty of other people wanting to make different choices. Nevertheless, a church that says, do this, believe that, follow my exact directives, and God will "cover you with his umbrella of mercy," or some such solicitous guarantee, will find people of that need attending.

Still other auditors go about looking for a faith communion that will give them an authentic voice but allow them room to think for themselves! We have a world full of frightened people looking for a substitute parent but we also have just as many, perhaps many more, who are saying, Give it to me straight but then give me room and don't manipulate me.

Many years ago Dr. Carlyle Marney, the late great Southern Baptist preacher and pastoral counselor, came to Gainesville, Florida for a preaching mission at First Baptist Church. I went down one morning for a breakfast session with Dr. Marney. I was particularly anxious to hear him because, better than most, he understood the emotional dimension of faith and choice. The hall was full of Baptist ministers, Carlyle Marney, and me. A decade later I still distinctly recall two specific things Dr. Marney said that early morning. .

The first thing was, "We are Baptist not by theology but by temperament." That's true of each one of us! You are an Episcopalian, not because Episcopal beliefs are different, but because you are temperamentally an Episcopalian. She is Roman Catholic, not because she reads a different Bible but because this suit fits. He is Baptist not because Baptists have a corner on the gospel but because he is a Baptist. Pentecostals are Pentecostals because they are temperamentally Pentecostals.

The second thing I recall Dr. Marney saying had everyone pointing at me and giving me a very friendly chiding. Marney said, "If you attend a Church of God you hear the minister say, 'GOD says.' If you attend a Church of Christ you will hear the minister saying, 'CHRIST says.' If you attend a Baptist Church you will hear the minister say, 'The BIBLE says.' If you attend a Methodist Church," he continued, "you will hear the minister say, 'It seems to *me.*' . . . "!

Everyone pointed at me and roared with laughter. Then, when things quieted down, Dr. Marney then said, "But never forget this also. Until you, as a minister of the gospel, can say 'it seems to *ME,*' your faith is not really your own!"

That's precisely where modern-day United Methodists have a wide open opportunity to evangelize, truly reach unnumbered millions of today's people with our message from God. As John Wesley said two hundred years ago (and I paraphrase for clarity's sake): Only two things are required of a person to become a Methodist—a desire to know Christ *personally* and the will to think and *let think!*

Another factor giving shape to the message is the leader. As we look at the list of reasons why people are filling churches, one becomes quickly aware that leadership is a common denominator. Each pastor, whatever his/her motivation, gives clear and decisive leadership! Therefore, it is pointed out, people are not looking for content as much as they are looking for deliberate and decisive containers. Marshall McLuhan was right all along, "The medium is the message." *Pray God your leader gets the message right!"*

Such reflections on why some churches are full and others, even where a great gospel is lovingly preached, remain empty is given further credibility by a cursory look at a sample list of leaders. Today, people are responding to Billy Graham, Bob Schuller, Sun Myung Moon, Jimmy Swaggart, Bhagwan Shree Rajneesh, Ernest Ainsley, and Norman Vincent Peale—just to give a sampling of the better known crowd gatherers. What do they have in common? Not the message but leadership!

Take another sampling. Look around your own community and identify the churches with full parking lots and full pews. The message given throughout every church in your community may even be the same. But some churches are growing and others are simply groaning. Why? The same reason. Growing churches have real leadership, and holding or dwindling churches have caretakers. The growing church has a minister; the holding church has a chaplain.

Therefore, we are looking for a leader, motivated by the love and compassion of God, sharing his or her special message from God, and doing so in a specific, decisive, and compassionate way. These are the people who are seeing the masses respond.

Here decisive, invitational evangelism becomes so important in understanding the real nature of church growth. And, this is where The United Methodist Church, among others, is losing out today. We tend, with many magnificent exceptions, to shoot from the hip, to use a scatter gun. We often proclaim a message geared to please everyone and address no one. We shoot at everything and aim at nothing. Other churches, those experiencing the by-product of growth, are using a rifle and are aiming from the shoulder. They are targeting their constituents and inviting them to come and get rich, become healed, speak in tongues, have better mental health, or whatever the market they may want to exploit.

Declining churches need also to "target" and share a legitimate specific message steeped in prayer, preparation, and integrity. We must have a message and invite people to do something about that message. Then, ask our listeners to say, Yes, No, or Wait in response to our personal and practical proclamation. We must give leadership and be decisive. We must be leaders and be invitational!

There are people milling around our towns and cities today who do not want to be spoon-fed. They don't believe for a minute that accepting certain doctrines and tithing to some "one true church" will make them healthy, wealthy, and wise. They are desperately looking for a church which targets them, saying, "Give yourself a chance to have a personal, intelligent, demanding, meaningful relationship with Christ and, when you have done that, keep using your own mind and encourage others to do the same." Each United Methodist church in this country that is sharing its unique message of nonmanipulated surrender to Christ and the continued use of the mind (pluralism, tolerance, etc.) is probably growing in significant numbers.

We must come to understand that people are going about making legitimate choices today about what churches meet their needs, if not actually auditing their proclamation in accordance with their need category, and many are saying, "Give us more churches that proclaim good sense to people like us. Give us people who want faith, even a costly faith, but do not want to have to give up their brains!" We must understand this about the nature and dynamics of church growth.

The Trust Factor

One policy that continues to hurt the United Methodist denomination is the tendency to run the modern church within the confines of a horse and buggy mentality. On the American frontier a minister was given an appointment with the knowledge that he would be in that particular charge two, three, or perhaps four years. This was a good approach for that day, a day of highly stable communities and villages, a day where continuity of spirit and society was maintained by the community itself. The minister could come and go, and knew that would be the case. He knew he would be unable to settle in and get comfortable. Even if he were not so inclined, he would of necessity be required to get back to work— hit the ground running.

Today, everything is different except the bureaucratic mentality. Like the British at Omdurman or Balaklava, our bureaucracy charges into the modern era, seemingly oblivious to its new firearms and breach-loaded artillery, believing that short-term itineracy, like the cavalry, will always have an honored place on the field of battle. In fact, we are fond of saying that the commitment to short-term pastorate is the mark of a faithful minister. We hold to the idea that someone "who is part of the iteneracy," someone who will live with us in the past, is a true and faithful servant of the order. And, many local pastors join the bureaucracy in this mentality. They do so because they know it is easier to move as old sermons run out. Also, many see short-term itineracy as a good way to get into position to climb the next rung of the ladder without having to do it where they are currently assigned. The mood of the seventeenth and eighteenth century was, "Give us variety for we have none!" The twentieth century cries, "Give us stability for we have none!"

Show me one church, of any denomination, that is vital, growing, and burning the world up for Christ, where the minister has not enjoyed the luxury and privilege of long-term involvement! I have been in hundreds of churches, worked in several dozen conferences all across the nation. I can't name one! On the other hand, I can name numerous churches that are alive, prosperous, missional, socially involved, and growing like a weed. In these churches the minister has had time and occasion to win trust and bring stability.

He or she has grown weary of hearing someone say, "I sure would like to move to your church, but I know you won't be here long, so I guess I'll stay where I am." They have become embarrassed by the mentality that says stay here three or four years, don't rock the boat, and then move up to "a better appointment." These pastors sense the need to succeed where they are, or they don't deserve a better appointment. They are saying, "Give me a chance to compete from a solid and stable base!" They are saying, "Move me if you need me, but don't move me just to be moving me!"

By giving the pastor a stable place of ministry, the church can become the place of trust, continuity, and stability. In this atmosphere, the preacher can extend an invitation which motivates.

3. THE NATURE OF MOTIVATION

One of the great people and colorful characters of The United Methodist Church was the late Dr. Glenn "Tex" Evans, who served on the Board of Discipleship during the late Sixties. Tex was a great storyteller, and whenever he returned from an assignment he drew the rapt attention of the entire staff. One day Tex came in from a trip and shared the following story.

He had just returned to the office from a preaching mission somewhere on the eastern shore of Maryland. He had been preaching in an old church where the first Methodist bishop, Francis Asbury, had once preached. Tex said he was standing in front of the church with one of its members, and both were admiring the beautiful river that ran by just below the hill in front of the old church. "All of a sudden," Tex said, "my friend turned to me and said, 'Brother Evans, when Bishop Asbury came out here to preach his first sermon, that river was swollen and clogged with broken ice! Brother Evans,' he continued, 'Do you want to know *how* Bishop Asbury managed to cross that flooded river?'" Tex looked at him and said, "No, I'd like for you to think about *why* he would cross that flooded and frozen river!"

How we do a good thing isn't nearly as important as *why* we do it. What motivates a person to be a servant of God carries more critical content than what method one uses in this service. Motive validates method. Thus we study motivation prior to explaining the nuts and bolts of a method, the evangelistic invitation. We not only need to look at motivation in its specific application, the invitation, but also in its general application, the ministry.

Why am I in ministry? I often go over a list of potential motivational factors I discovered in Emory Griffin's book, *The Mind Changers*. When I look at this list of possibilities, I am reminded that many of us fit certain combinations within this list, though most of us predominantly fit one of these options. Personally, I try to keep up with my motivational instincts because I want to keep health and integrity in my ministry. Griffin gives us these basic categories:

The Non-Lover: This person doesn't try to persuade. His or her motto is "live and let live." Execute your duty and expedite your exit!

16

The Flirt: These are persons who have love but have more of it for themselves than for others. Their "evangelism" has pathological overtones. They are like cowboys looking for a showdown, or Fonzie cooing for a girl. They need another notch in their belt because they need another notch in their belt.

The Seducer: These individuals are characterized by a sense of seduction in their proclamation. They are motivated by the means which justify the end. They promise that, if you will believe what they say and do as they say, you will become: the starting quarterback, a business success, the head of the company, or Miss Cucumber of Periwinkle County.

The Rapist: Rapists are motivated because "anything's fair in love or war"! They use force, coercion, and other forms of highly charged emotional environments.

The Smother Lover: This option motivates persons who love and smother you to death. Their personal needs are of such a kind and quality that they are unwilling to take no for an answer. They recognize no such thing as free choice because their needs require constant assurance of "success."

The Legalist: Some persuade with a sense of obligation or duty. They have to do it or "burn in hell," and they are not about to allow you to do that to them! This paradox is a primary reason for much of today's very unloving fundamentalism.

The True Lover: This one is loving and just. The true lover cares more about others than self. True lovers respect human rights. Though they may be saddened by your choice, they are willing to let you say no.

I fit one of these options as well as a disconcerting residue of one or two other types of love hidden here or there! I want to stay in touch with what really motivates me because staying in touch is the primary way I have of getting healthy and of staying healthy.

In this interest, we examine the nature of motivation from the standpoint of our *initial* motivation, our *limited* motivation and, the all-important factor of *replenished* motivation. Having laid this last stone— *why* do people serve in ministry and *what* compels them to extend invitations—we can begin looking at the practical methodology inherent in the decisive, nonmanipulative, evangelistic invitation.

My Initial Motivation

The initial motive is perhaps the most important reflection of the three. Who called me in the first place? What compelled me to take up this difficult, arduous, rewarding, maddening vocation?

Behavioral psychologists tell us that occupational choices tend to be based on early childhood needs. For instance, they suggest that the primary factor motivating people who select medicine for a vocation is an inherent fear of pain. Most physicians enter the field because they want to prevent pain if at all possible. That's not a bad motivation. I enjoy the thought of having a doctor who has an intrinsic fear of pain, but I would also want that doctor to know that was his/her motivation. Then, he or she would be even more effective!

Other doctors are motivated to enter medicine because of the money, prestige, and position. In some cases, the potential doctor has experienced inadequacy and low self-esteem, thus fostering deep need within to become some kind of god. All doctors need to check out their motivation to fully understand why they extend an invitation to others for healing.

It is common knowledge that many people who go into psychology or psychiatry do so because they hurt, have been hurt, are hurting, or have had a need for understanding all their lives! These often are our best counselors, but only if they know what is behind their choice, if they know what motivates them to excel in this area, if they have turned their lemon into a lemonade. Then they can meaningfully invite me to come in for help.

So it is with the ministry, particularly the preaching ministry! I need to discern, as best I can, who or what called me so that invitation has veracity and vitality!

Some of us may discover we are like the young man I met some time ago who said, "I left the ministry because my mother called me to the ministry in the first place." Hurrah for him! He should leave the ministry and feel good about his new job which honors his personhood and social responsibility.

Still other preachers may be like a young man I met during my seminary years. He was a very likable person, and I enjoyed being around him. However, an uneasy question came through his personality. Why is this person entering the ministry in the first place? There was obvious reason for such a choice. The way he talked, lived, worked, and acted shouted for resolution of the same question. Finally one day, having become his friend, I said, "Tell me. Why are you going into the ministry?" His immediate answer was, "Because it's the only job I can think of where you don't have to work very hard if you don't want to, and you are someone important the minute you move into a community." I never knew where this kind of motivation led my acquaintance, but hopefully and ultimately it led him into some other kind of work.

Motivation is important to understand why I am here, who I am in this job, and what I am about in this work. I know of a case, for instance, of a devout young woman who wanted more than anything in the world to be a nun somewhere in South America. She got her wish, and soon her world collapsed around her. Her invitation to others to come to the Wedding Feast of our Lord became a weeping fit, and she came home seriously ill. After much psychiatric treatment she was finally able to admit that she had chosen her occupation, in the first place, because of a deep-seated fear of sex!

An acquaintance once confided in me that he was going as a missionary to Africa because "his ego couldn't compete with the rest of his seminary buddies if they should get ahead of him in their careers." Needless to say, he was not in Africa long. Going out, anywhere, to invite others is validated by the veracity of motivation.

I once *volunteered* for an inner-city church and was not very effective. It was a wonderful old church with many marvelous people, but I was a square peg in a round hole! Later I discovered that the primary reason for this obvious misfit was the motivational aspect of my initial volunteering. I had unknowingly requested the assignment for two basic reasons: (1) I felt guilty about being in suburbia and reasoned that I needed to "serve my time"; and (2) I felt my peers would think I was unusually dedicated to make such a move! I was impressed with myself and felt sure they would be even more so.

It did not work out well. I suffered. My family suffered. The church survived me mainly because it was a gracious and tough church which knew who had called it. This church knew it stood to be a lighthouse for the living God. Having that same sense of motivation and clarity is what I've worked toward ever since!

Why are we serving? Who called us? Why are we here?

Some years ago I occasionally spoke with the head football coach at The University of Florida. He was in his first year and had not yet won a single game. One day I said, "Coach! Anybody who would be a head football coach *or* a minister, is either called of God and has absolutely no choice, or he is a fool! I know what my excuse is, but I'm not sure what yours is!" After a few moments the coach looked at me and said, "I think I'm some kind of fool!"

Any of us who face the tough schedule, the demanding routines, the peaks and valleys, the thrill of victory and the agony of defeat, faced by ministers or coaches, must know without a shadow of doubt that God has called us and we have no real choice but to follow God and give God our best! This calling must be our motivation!

Our Limited Motivation

I am convinced that the clergy of any denomination that grants "defacto tenure" must go considerably beyond their initial motivation. Some pastors who serve in denominations where we are sent and not called, transferred and not fired, and whose job is protected by church law—those of us who minister in such situations, which expose us so readily to our own human frailties—must recognize the fact that with this "defacto tenure" we have *limited* motivation. I can be the laziest minister in town or the hardest working, and *all* depends on me, my choices, and my good sense to rely constantly on God.

In a Baptist church, where there is no tenure, defacto or otherwise, the minister is doubly motivated! He has the motivation of his calling plus the motivation of his church. The Baptist minister must paint or get off the ladder! If he hasn't doubled attendance, and purchased fourteen new buses by the end of his second year, his job may be on the line! If church membership is declining, his future is very uncertain.

In systems using defacto tenure this is not the case. Ministers serving in this kind of system can wait it out, be careful not to rock the boat, keep things together, and await a "better opportunity" further up the ladder!

Nontenured clergy must make their own situations good and meaningful and alive. Defacto tenured clergy can, if they so desire, wait around until something more deserving of them falls into their laps. Pastors with defacto tenure fully know that even if they don't do a real day's work and the church remains dead, and they are not promoted, the odds favor that they will at least remain on their present level and they will not be forced to slide back down the corporate ladder.

Defacto tenure, protected ministers, a system that asks "what is best for the pastor and not what is best for the church," has played havoc with The United Methodist Church. The clergyperson of this church who would function meaningfully and significantly within the system must come to grips with this systemic handicap! Or, the system must change! The system must finally and ultimately ask what is best for this church, not this pastor. This change could be a great thing for the church, and it could mean equally as much to the pastor. The pastor will then be on the same footing which most of the work force enjoys: namely, full motivation, driven from within and pressured from without.

I have often asked this question in pastor's schools or retreats for ministers. We accept the fact that our church is currently in decline and all our leaders are admonishing us to become "more evangelistic." It's still not happening. What would happen throughout our church if today, somehow, there came down a General Conference resolution that said, Show vital, healthy church growth by the end of the year or prepare to be demoted! What would happen? Things would begin to change immediately.

For example, I have heard much about the great African revival. And, I know that the Methodist Church of Kenya is part of the revival. Most pastors within that system serve circuits of from thirty to fifty churches! How are they doing it? The statistics are unbelievable! In the year 1900, for instance, the colony of Kenya had a population of ten million people out of which a mere five thousand professed to being Christians. When I went out to Kenya in 1976, the nation of Kenya then had a population of twelve million people out of which eight million were Christians! It was really happening, throughout all the churches of east Africa.

In exploring the difference, wherever I went, I asked this question of the leaders: If you have a minister who simply is not doing the job, nothing's happening, and the work is not going forward, how do you handle it over here? Bishop Johson Komoro gave me this answer, "We have a firm, two-step policy: first we go to the pastor, try to help him identify why the job is not getting done, and work out a plan of action; second, if things do not change after that, we then return to his charge and ask for his credentials."

I sometimes wish I had such whole motivation rather than limited motivation. I sometimes wish I served in a church that would make me paint or get off the ladder. It seems so much easier, given my human frailties and inherent laziness. In lieu of that, however, I must recognize the problem of limited motivation, and I must do something about it myself!

Replenishing Motivation

The more I study the lives of the men and women who presented their ministry with courage and steadfastness, the more I become impressed with the way they did it: personal prayer life and devotion. They stayed in touch with the Source. They continually replenished their motivation.

When my youngest son went away to seminary, and took his first church, a student pastorate, he asked me what was the single most important thing he could do. I told him, above and beyond anything else, keep your prayer life intact! Keep in touch.

Ironically, this is usually the first thing to go. I know this has been true in my life. I have had to fight that battle, come back from lameness and lifelessness, time and time again. I have always been a very busy pastor, and I have always had trouble with my devotional life. Not only has my busy schedule pushed "secondary things" to the background, but I periodically and sporadically find reading my Bible a dreary discipline. My times of prayer occasionally are bouts with doubts, soiled thoughts, wandering mind, watching the clock and saying to myself, "I wonder if I've been here long enough so I can now get up!"

Nevertheless, getting back from vacant to victorious, from empty to energized has always come through *replenishment.* I see that vital ministry is not a high-powered car that must stop at an occasional garage to purchase a new battery. Vital ministry is more like a golf cart that must be recharged daily or it grinds to a halt. The golf cart may look good, add to the scenery, and provide a good place to get out of the sun, but it is wasted if it does not work right. Just like the golf cart, I need regular energizing and find this true among all of God's vital servants!

As part of my devotion, I was recently rereading a favorite book, Helmut Thielicke's *Encounter with Spurgeon* (p. 6). Thielicke says about Spurgeon,

> It is characteristic of the nature of his preaching ministry that, despite the turbulence of a successful life in which he was surrounded by crowds of people, he did not allow himself to become swamped with externals and consumed with busyness. Instead, he immersed himself in the quietness of prayer and meditation, receptively filling his mind and soul, and then went forth recreated from these quiet hours to pour himself out without reserve.

Spurgeon teaches the lesson that Richard Cecil shared with ministers almost one hundred years earlier. Cecil said, "The leading deficit in Christian ministry is want of a devotional habit." Thomas Hooker said even more clearly, "Prayer is my chief work, and it is by means of it that I carry on the rest."

Of all the materials on this important subject, William Graham Scroggie's statement has convicted, convinced, and redirected me more than any other. Scroggie once wrote, "It is when preachers become popular that they are in greatest danger of neglecting prayer; but it was when man most sought Christ that he most sought God." Then Scroggie goes on to add this zinger. "One may preach *well* without praying much if he but have the intellectual and oratorical gifts, but no one can preach *effectually* (that is, possessing the power and ability to effect people and things) without praying much, for effectual preaching depends more on grace than on gifts" (from *Daily Notes*, The Scripture Union, Toronto, July 21, 1955).

How desperately I continually need to read that great statement! It isn't that I am so popular but that I am so easily contented with taking my meager gifts and getting by. Most people seem to like what I do and how I do it. They are regularly telling me that they appreciate my practical messages, or my sense of humor, or "something." God has called us to make a difference, to be hooked up to the power, and to become the channel of that power. God has summoned us to effect and not affect. He has asked us to move mountains while constantly reminding us "I am the vine, you are the branches . . . apart from me you can do nothing" (John 15:5).

Bishop Quayle of Kansas once put it in such a beautiful way. The bishop said,

> Preaching is the art of making a sermon and delivering it. *Why no,* that is not preaching. Preaching is the art of making a *preacher* and delivering *that.* Preaching is the outrush of soul in speech. Therefore, the elemental business in preaching is not with the preaching, but with the preacher. What then, in the light of this, is the task of a preacher? Mainly this: the amassing of a great soul so as to have something worthwhile to give. The sermon is the preacher up to date.

Consequently, replenishing my motivation is a concern of significant and practical consequence. Even if God has called me and that call is my chief motivation, and, even if I give my pastoral appointment all I have, whether the church authorities hold me responsible or not, even then, I must stay in touch, keep in contact, and regularly replenish my motivation.

Then, when my motivation is as right and healthy as it can possibly be, and it is as charged as daily contact with the Source can provide, then, and only then am I ready to extend an invitation that has integrity and validity! I have a word supported by a life. I have an ethic corroborated by an ethos. I have a valid message to share and now a valid invitation to extend!

4. DEFINITION: EVANGELISM AND INVITATION

Because these two terms, *evangelism* and *invitation,* are so highly charged in emotional content, to say nothing of being so abused and misused, we need to define our words. We need to be sure we are talking about the same things. And, we must define them within the same framework because *evangelism* and *invitation* are simultaneously inner related and mutually inclusive.

Evangelism

We must discontinue interpreting *evangelism* as either an emotional binge left over from the sawdust trail or as getting new people to join the church. One view, the gospel of the sawdust trail, was born on the American frontier and was relatively unknown before the Charles Finney revivals of the early nineteenth century. The other interpretation of evangelism, that of getting people to join the church, came primarily from Calvinistic theology which, from the very outset, equated joining with "profession of faith."

In our effort to define "evangelism" more accurately we often try to go back to the roots of the gospel. And, the need to do this is part of the problem! When people around our churches say such things as, "We need to get back to that old-time religion," they usually do not mean Jesus, Paul, Peter, or even Luther, Knox, or Wesley! They mean grandmother or Aunt Clarabelle! They mean those most readily influenced by The Second Great Awakening! They want to get back to the rather familiar turf of this great American revival phenomenon. In defining evangelism, they do not usually want to go all the way back to the source of the concept. Albert C. Outler (*Evangelism in the Wesleyan Spirit,* p. 76) wrote, "The mindset of the Second Great Awakening, which still seems to some the faith once for all delivered to the saints, will have to be *transcended* (not to be confused with *jettisoned*)." Grandmother saw an evangelism that was a stroke of genius for her times. It seemed, and perhaps was, directed by the Holy Spirit to touch and reach the tough frontiersmen of that day. And, we want to affirm that relevant methodology of the period, but we also want to transcend that methodology.

24

Jesus, quite different from his later disciples, seems to define evangelism in a much more eternal, far-reaching context. His manifestation of the concept seems more elastic and unconditional. The term itself is a Greek word, *euangelistes,* and the word originally meant simply "a messenger of good." Correspondingly, I always define the term as someone who "brings the Good News of God to the agony of humankind." This makes evangelism virtually apply to *anything* in which the healing, helpful word of God is brought to bear on humankind's hurting, loneliness, or need of salvaging in *whatever* the area may be: social, personal, relational, ecological, and so on. A person who participates in evangelism is a person who helps bring the Good News of God to the agony of humankind!

By this definition, all preaching should be evangelistic! For, if what I am saying does not represent the healing word from God concerning the bleeding agonies of people, why bother, as a minister of the gospel, to say it anyway? Why claim to be a preacher of the Good Word from God? Why take up people's valuable time? As Margaret Chaplain Anderson wrote so tersely and so profoundly in her book, *A Wail from a Distressed Soul,*

> Oh preacher, holy man, hear my heart weeping: I long to stand and shout my protest: Where is your power and where is your message? Where is the gospel of mercy and love? Your words are nothingness, nothingness, nothingness. We who have come to listen are betrayed. Servant of God, I am bitter and desolate. What do I care for perfection of phrases? Cursed be your humor, your poise, your diction. See how my soul turns to ashes within me? You who have vowed to declare your redeemer, *give me the words that would save!*

So, I attempt to move on and move out to true evangelism. I seek to synthesize God's love and human need so that I am now an evangelist and therefore evangelistic.

Evangelism, by definition, is not reaching people at the point of your agenda for their lives. True evangelism is endeavoring to bring God's healing word to their lives, whatever their broken or disrupted agenda.

Invitation

If endeavoring to bring the Good News of God to the agony of humankind is true evangelism, then the "invitation" is but a logical, sequential request for people to *do something* about the proclamation of the hour. It is but a decisive effort to grant the auditor the opportunity to say "yes," "no," or "maybe" concerning the question of the moment. This right of the auditor to answer will prevent us from confusing "invitation" with "mandate." One of the reasons "invitation" has fallen into such disrepute is primarily because we hear people giving *mandates* but calling them *invitations*. The two are obviously quite different.

For instance, if I invite you to my home I am simply being decisive in our friendship and offering you options on how you may wish to respond to my invitation. As it is an invitation, you can come or not, accept or reject. Mandates leave no such options! You do what I say, or God will get you for turning me down.

Jesus did not give mandates. Jesus extended invitations! He did not hum fifty-seven verses of "Just as I Am" until someone finally gave up, came down, and did what he/she was required to do. Jesus extended invitations! He simply walked along the fields and lakes saying, "Come, follow me" and kept right on going!

Can you recall what the service of Jesus Christ is all about? He said, "You take up your cross and follow me" (Matt. 16:24), and he was an inviter! What he did made sense, was sequential and complemented the time he had spent in teaching by encouraging people to do something about it and at least consider doing it now!

John Wesley leaves no evidence that he ever extended a mandate. Quite the contrary, if you read his Journal carefully, you will find page after page with notations something like this, "Today I preached at Bristol. I offered them the Word of God and left praying that God's Spirit would bring forth much fruit."

Christ asks us together to bring God's love to human need and give human beings nonmanipulative opportunity to do what they are willing to do about that need and the answer to that need. We then leave it there, thankful that the Holy Spirit will continue to minister, and we ride away saying with Wesley, "I pray that God's Spirit will bring forth much fruit."

In defining *invitation,* we speak of a logical, sequential opportunity to accept, reject, or hold in abeyance one's proclamation of good news. The invitation does not presuppose a specific response, but confronts the listener with the necessity of dealing with that moment's offering. And such an invitation, to be truly valid, must be sequential, that is, it must follow logically from the offering.

For example, if I preach this Sunday on God's good news for the cancer of racial injustice, an appropriate invitation would encourage people to look hard at the subject *right now* (how this can be done is the subject of Chapter 9). On the other hand, if I preach on the race issue and extend my ambiguous, all-purpose "Invitation to Christian Discipleship," I am probably being nonsequential and therefore irrelevant. The prejudiced or bigoted church member sitting in the congregation, found in abundance throughout the land, is most probably already a member of the church and is subsequently relieved of any pressure brought on by the ministry of the Holy Spirit during the morning proclamation. "After all," this member reasons, "I'm already a member of the church and that's all this crazy preacher is inviting me to do about his annoying sermon!" The bigot is obligingly eased out of the service, and little else is apt to occur.

The conclusion of the service must be invitational and the invitation must be logical and sequential. The same principle is true when we, as a matter of rote, ritual, or ridiculousness, simply urge people to come forward and repent. Chances are fair that the person has already been converted at heart, but not in attitude toward other persons. There must occur a logical invitation that deals with the message and the moment. A sequential invitation literally confronts the proclamation and the auditor. For instance, given a message on human relations or on initial conversion, the hour would be much better concluded by asking the congregation to bow their heads and "make their pew an altar of prayer." The minister could simply say, "Maybe you are here this morning and you have never surrendered your own inadequacies to God and are thus dependent on hostilities toward races for support and assurance. Will you surrender this in prayer right here, right now, as you sit in silence?" You are not dictating a specific response, mandating an acceptable reaction, you are (1) extending a sequential invitation and (2) presenting a logical opportunity for possible response.

If we preach on missions, let us extend an opportunity that will enable our listeners to respond to a new awakening concerning missions. If we preach on stewardship, then the invitation should flow logically from the premise of that sermon. If we speak on family relations, then family relations; on prayer, then prayer; on service, then let us submit a soft, confrontational experience that is sequential.

In our effort to define the term *invitation* we are also caught up in the larger question of defining the problem inherent with *not* inviting. This problem is simply a matter of integrity.

For instance, are we being honest, to say nothing of reasonable, if we profess to care, spend day after day and hour after hour, service after service, and never once ask anyone to accept or reject the specific proposal that we claim to care so deeply about? No one else in our time is allowed to communicate with such glaring discrepancy! If you sell cars and believe in your product or are committed to its value, then you are *expected* to eventually say, "Will you buy?" By endeavoring to persuade without granting an honest *opportunity* to respond is a failure of integrity, to say nothing of a travesty of stewardship.

The minister faces this same expectancy. Therefore, the pastor must carefully evaluate his/her proclamation at this point. Am I saying anything worthy of response? If so, then the opportunity to do so should be inauspiciously or conspicuously granted. On the other hand, if I am not saying anything worthy of response, maybe I should cease interacting with the busy lives of the people I am supposedly serving.

The description of completeness is also part of the larger problem of integrity. We are not being truly honest when our preaching can best be described as "run on" and never culminates in any meaningful decisiveness. If someone is persuading me to buy a car, I want the wheels with it. If someone gives me a novel to read, I would like to have the last chapter intact.

People want the entire package! One summer, when my parsonage committee replaced an exterior door on my residence but failed to have it painted, I had the same feeling of incompleteness and frustration many congregations might feel on Sunday morning when the service ends so unfinished, so indecisively.

Not only does any congregation with average intelligence discern the incompleteness of the hour, they also sense the lethalness of that discrepancy. They know, or sense, that what the pastor has done, or failed to do, has killed one of the very goals of the worship experience—response. Without granting the opportunity to respond, we are dead and do not even know it!

We are also talking about the problem of simple and sequential logic because the world in which we are required to function is oriented, rightly or wrongly, around "pitch and response." The people where we work know fully that if a salesman is promoting Firestone tires he will ultimately and logically ask you to say "yes" or "wait" to his expenditure of time. And, by that same token, no person, outside the pulpit, that is, spends twenty-five minutes trying to sell a vacuum cleaner and then says "Thank you so much for the fellowship. Let's go home!" Nor does another person spend thirty minutes trying to sell you a lawn mower and then say, at the very last moment, "Do you want to buy a car or not?"

Invitations are *expected* in our culture. People do not want to be pressured, but they know something is wrong if they are not given the chance to make a decision.

Therefore, *evangelism* is studying, praying, and working hard to bring the Good News of God to the agony of humankind. The "invitation" is but the logical sequence of this presentation.

It is the process of a loving, prayerful, prepared minister saying, "Here is what I believe to be God's Good News for our need, this day. Will you say 'yes,' 'no,' or 'maybe' to this Good News right now?"

5. PRINCIPLES OF DECISIVE PREACHING

This desperately needed and much coveted leadership, this decisiveness in preaching is predicated on three basic principles: the principle of *proclaimer,* the principle of *proclamation,* and the principle of *concretion.* Understanding and utilizing the primary principles of decisiveness are vital to decisive preaching.

The Proclaimer

God's message to us in our agony or lostness speaks for itself. However, if the medium, the conveyer of that message, makes or breaks that message, in actual effect becomes the message, then the care and feeding of the proclaimer becomes essential. This is precisely why the proclaimer him or herself becomes the priority point of focus in this reflection on decisiveness in ministry. As Spurgeon once said, "To go into the pulpit with the listless air of those gentlemen who loll about, and lean upon the cushion as if they had at last reached a quiet resting place, is, I think, most censurable."

Concerning the part the proclaimer plays in decisiveness, Spurgeon once said, "If I were asked, 'What in a Christian minister is the most essential quality for securing success in winning souls for Christ?' and if I were asked a second or a third time, I should not vary the answer, for personal observation drives me to the conclusion that, as a rule, real success is proportionate to the preacher's earnestness . . . in many instances ministerial success is traceable almost entirely to an intense zeal . . . an eager enthusiasm in the cause of God" (Theilicke, *Encounter with Spurgeon,* p. 81).

After almost thirty years as a pastor I see the whole dynamic of interaction as one would view a game of billiards. I am not willing to sink this metaphor into a hole but certainly see validity in the law of physics which reminds us that the velocity of an object transfers *proportionately* upon impact. In other words, the cue ball moves the triangle of balls in direct relationship to its velocity. If the cue ball (the local pastor as the moving leadership force) simply drifts down the table, its contact with the triangle (representing not people who need to be pushed about and dropped in this or that hole but rather ideas, problems, needs, and circumstances within the church desperately needing to be addressed) will result in very little movement of anything. The ball may finally end up mired down in the middle of the mass, enjoying the idea of "great fellowship," but nothing useful or dynamic is taking place.

On the other hand, if the ball is smashed down the table like a runaway train, with too much drive or velocity, then everything on the table which needs adequate and sensible handling can be blown all over the room! Again, this is where motivation becomes such a great factor! People who are too driven, too pushy, too determined to have it their way, usually manifest some personal need that renders them fanatical at worst and feverish at best. They end up unfulfilled and unfulfilling. As Bishop Arthur G. Moore used to say, "A fanatic is not someone with too much religion but someone with too little sense."

As is true in most cases, real leadership (decisiveness) comes somewhere at the synthesis between these two extremes. Decisive ministry in the congregation takes place at the point of what Spurgeon calls *earnestness*. Decisive ministry begins to happen when the local pastor cares deeply, believes ardently and wants, with all his/her heart, to see things happen for the cause of Christ!

While in seminary I served a student charge in central Georgia, the Shady Dale Circuit. One night I was present at a district minister's meeting at First Church Covington. I was sitting next to a close friend whose country circuit was near my own. He had done, rather God had done through him, a most remarkable job in the two and one-half short years my friend had been in his charge. I knew the story well. When Dan had been assigned this remote circuit of four rural churches, one was barely surviving, one had burned down, and the district superintendent who had appointed him sent him to the charge with instructions to close the other two!

By the time of our meeting that particular night, the surviving church was much stronger, the burned down church was larger and stronger than the first church, one of the two churches that was scheduled to be closed was growing slightly and the second of those two churches had gone from one Sunday service each month to a service every Sunday, plus a brand new Sunday school! Not only that, all four churches had developed a strong mission program, were all well over their budgets and had just been named one of the top rural circuits of the North Georgia Conference for that particular year!

At the evening meeting the district superintendent commented on this remarkable turn of events and then turned to my friend and said, "Dan, tell us how you were able to do it!"

I will never forget the confusion that swept over Dan's face. He knew very well what the superintendent wanted. He wanted a list of new committees, kits ordered from headquarters, and unique strategies employed to accomplish such a feat. Dan stuttered, stammered, and finally said nothing. Dan did not know how it happened, and I did not figure it out until days later. What had happened was really quite simple and elemental. Dan went into that church with a great, heartfelt *earnestness!* He cared about the people, their faith, their churches, their mutual mission to the world, and God used this compassion to infect the whole lot of them! Once again, it was the leaven affecting the whole lump!

By granting the utter and final importance of the ministry of the Holy Spirit, and how true and necessary is the doctrine of the priesthood of all believers, the fact still remains—the pastor in the black robe or blue suit should be the *prime mover!* If he or she is not moved, the congregation is not going to move! If the pastor manifests no genuine earnestness, the parishioners tend to follow the leader (or lack of leading). Besides reminding us again of the importance of our devotional life, this principle of velocity transference has to be, in part, what D. Elton Trueblood had in mind when he observed, "Congregations do not *tend* to rise above the devotional level of their ministers."

Under the ministry of the Holy Spirit, the proclaimer is the catalytic agent. As the catalyst I want to know: Do I go about my work with genuine enthusiasm? Can something happen to those about me because it is happening to me!? Am I in earnest about my important task?

The Proclamation

The principle of *proclamation* is equally imperative. What is the proclaimer saying that is worthy of response? Am I *saying* anything that really matters? Just as there cannot be commitment without something worthy of commitment, there also cannot be decisiveness in ministry without decisive proclamation!

I would not be so pretentious at this point as to describe my own theology as "proclamation worth response." While my understanding of God and the divine Word for the world is certainly sacred to me, we are reminded that each of us has benefited from a special message or direction from God. In sharing that special message, with enthusiasm and with bold leadership, we know God will use us and bless us in our varied and respective tasks. For the sake of decisive proclamation, how-ever—while admitting the condition of many mainline denominations which need to return to a message worthy of response—I would much like to suggest these guidelines:

1. Is this message Christ-centered?

Though we try it very regularly, it is utter foolishness to talk about "Christianity" without talking about Christ! One thing this confused world does not need is just "ianity." We already have "ianity" and "ism" up to our eyeballs! What this agonized world needs is Christ, and we have always said that this is what we believe. As John Wesley said to Francis Asbury, who departed for the New World, "Offer them Christ."

In his Journal, August 4, 1786, Wesley penned these words, "I am not afraid that the people called Methodists should ever cease to exist either in Europe or America. But I am afraid, lest they should only exist as a dead sect, having the form of religion without the power." I have heard, and deeply appreciated, that quotation many times. The rest of that quotation, however, I have not heard nearly as often and the rest of that famous quotation is one of the critical messages, to the proclaimer, in our day. Wesley then said, "And this undoubtedly will be the case, unless they hold fast both the doctrine, spirit, and discipline with which they first set out." The decisive proclaimer must stay with the One who brought him/her.

Let me state the same thing in another way. I am convinced that much of the ideological and polarized struggle of our day centers not merely in our failure to lift up Christ but also in our illogical admonitions to *follow* and *serve* Christ without *knowing* Christ! This is an anachronistic faith.

To illustrate the concept of anachronism, we paraphrase a story from Louis Nizer in *My Life in Court*. Place yourselves in the rolling hill country of west central Kentucky on the night of February 2, 1809. The village doctor is summoned from his house in town to a small log cabin about five miles out in the country. A mother is about to give birth and the doctor is desperately needed.

After a long night of work the doctor returns wearily to his house, hitches up his horse, and drags himself through the front door. His wife, ever mindful of the need to be both attentive and interested, asks, "Well, how did it go?" "It was rough," replies the doctor, "but it was worth it! Do you know who was born this morning?" "No," responds his attentive wife, "Who?" And with an air of awe and wonder the doctor says, "Abraham Lincoln!" An anachronism is an event where the importance, sequence, or facts of the event are restructured or reinterpreted in light of later events or interpretations.

When we proclaim the Christian life without the Christ, growing up without being born, service without surrender, we are sowing weeds of frustration and discouragement in the lives of people. As Soren Kierkegaard once pointed out, it is one thing to become *a* Christian and another thing to *become* Christian. The former is a decision, the latter is a lifetime commitment.

We must get our life arranged according to the proper sequence. We do not endeavor to become Christian in order to become a Christian. This is anachronistic! This would be as illogical as asking someone to become a good husband in order to get married. The acceptable sequence is to get married and then become a good husband.

The case follows logically in faith. People become a Christian (decision) and enter into the process of becoming Christian (life commitment). The old evangelism told us that "conversion is the end of your faith." The new evangelism says, "True, but it is the front end!"

When we decide, through faith, to become a Christian we enter that process through the gate of Christ and then engage in the long-term task of becoming disciple, apostle, servant. With this sequence we have a foundation on which we can firmly stand. The polarity between "social action first" and "sloppy agape now" begins easily to dissolve in the smooth and reasonable flow of beginning with subjective peace (personal surrender) that results in objective unrest (adequate expression of our faith). If we begin with Christ then "ianity" becomes meaningful. It is the proclamation of "Ianitychrist" that is so bewildering today. What else would you expect? Reasonable people consider us suspect if we ask them to serve when they have not yet been exposed to the Savior.

Anachronistic proclamations have built-in frustrations and rampant futilities. But proclamations that *begin* with Christ can be decisive because they are rooted in power and lead much more easily to responsible engagements of the pressing social issues of our day.

2. Is what I am proclaiming gospel or propaganda?

A proclamation that makes one decisive, the subject of this chapter, is closely linked with the need to remember that people remain open to Good News but are not overly persuaded by pleas to save institutions that have grown irrelevant or meaningless. To be decisive, we the proclaimer must constantly ask whether this is gospel that I share, or whether it is evasive propaganda.

Dr. Leander Keck gives us wonderful help in separating the two. He defines *gospel* as that which we say on behalf of the need of the individual, regardless of the need of the institution. *Propaganda,* on the other hand, is that which we say on behalf of the need of the institution, regardless of the need of the individual.

Decisive proclaimers will discern the difference between gospel and propaganda. This discernment will not necessitate their choosing between the individual and the institution. It will force us, however, to care about the institution as a means of helping the individual. Such discernment will remind us that the only real way to save the institution is to be about the work for which the institution was intended!

Many years ago, before TV and VCR's, our leisure curiosity still enjoyed the feeding of numerous weekly magazines such as *Life, Collier's, Post,* and so on. I was working in my yard late one afternoon and was approached by a well-dressed young man carrying a briefcase and a big smile. He walked over to me and said, "I'd like to ask you a question!"

I naturally assumed he was a salesman of some variety but responded by saying, "Okay, ask!"

"What do you think of when you hear the word *Collier's?*", he said.

"I think of magazines," I replied.

"No," said he, "you should now think of encyclopedias, for Collier's has become a leading name in the world of encyclopedias." He then launched into a well-rehearsed proclamation of the value of owning a set of Collier's encyclopedias.

One late afternoon, about three weeks later, I was reading in the later afternoon in my living room. A well-dressed young man stepped to the door carrying a briefcase and a big smile. I walked over to the door, and he said immediately, "I'd like to ask you a question!"

I looked at him for a moment and said, "Okay, ask."

He said, "What do you think of when you hear the word *Collier's?*"

I said, "I think of encyclopedias."

He gasped, gulped, and shuffled his feet. "No, you should think of encyclopedias." He knew something was not quite right but could not exactly put his finger on it. Slightly recovered, but still in a daze, he then launched into the very same speech memorized by his *Collier's* teammate of a few days earlier. I stood there chagrined as he finished the recital in a daze. Then, he simply turned, walked out to the street and on up the road, still not sure what really happened back there. The young salesman was so preoccupied with the task of representing or saving the institution that he was totally oblivious to the need of the person he addressed!

When considering the principles of decisiveness, we desperately need to recall that real decisiveness is predicated on meeting needs. Our job is not to save the institution or even reach our sales quotas. Our job is to share the Good News of God at the point of human needs.

3. Am I concentrating on cause or symptom?

The old evangelism *announced*, "Look at what they're doing. Isn't that sinful?" An enlightened evangelism *asks*, "Why are they acting the way they're acting?" The latter recognizes the fact that sin is a symptom and not a cause. The enlightened proclaimer goes about the business of working on the causal factor, knowing full well that the symptoms will clear up on their own.

Doctors, if their leadership is adequate and decisive, follow the same guideline. A good doctor will study the symptoms of an individual as indicators of the malady.

Jesus shows us this principle throughout his ministry. He was not overly shocked by the adultery of the woman brought to him for stoning. He did not stone her, nor did he harangue her about her symptom. His concern was at the point of her separation from God, or the lack of respect she held for herself, or the gross unhappiness of her life that could drive her to such foolish indiscretion. He was always concerned with the *why* of an act, and through loving forgiveness he dealt with the *cause!*

One Sunday morning, as other worshipers filed through the door after the service, a stranger approached me and shook my hand. She stood there for a moment and finally spoke. She said, "I'm not a member of your church. In fact, this is my first Sunday to visit here. But, I would appreciate it very much if you would come visit my husband. Let me warn you," she continued, "he'll be very drunk and extremely abusive. He will call you every dirty name in the book. Please come, however. I think you may be able to help him." She slipped away after she gave me his name and their address.

I was able to drop by Wednesday of that week. And, everything happened as she said. I simply teased the man a bit and left without so much as having prayer, or leaving a tract. I continued to visit with him about once a week over the next several weeks. Gradually we began to establish a friendship. He was still drinking heavily and continued to call me interesting names, but now there was a faint smile on his face. Finally he began attending church and soon wanted to "do something." He decided he wanted to usher. I thought about it a bit and finally decided it would not hurt a thing, given the size of that sanctuary and the poor lighting, to have an usher with a bright red nose. Accordingly I both notified and warned the head usher. My new friend went to work as a regular usher.

One Sunday, following the morning service, he approached me and said, "Dean, I believe today I received Christ into my life in some kind of personal way, and I want to join this church." I received him into the church, and he continued to be a faithful church member (still drinking

heavily). Finally, after many months of caring, bridge-building, and re-
lentless attention *away* from his symptom, I decided to muster all the
brownie points I had gained in our friendship and pushed him to see a
psychiatrist. The psychiatrist referred him to a regular medical doctor,
and then the whole story came out. My friend had been in the first wave
on the assault at Normandy in World War II. He had been seriously
wounded by a shell explosion. Part of his skull was blown off. The army
hospital had replaced it with a stainless steel plate, and in the intervening
years the plate had slipped just enough to be an irritant to his brain. The
man was drinking (symptom) because he was living in pure hell (cause)!
He did not have a problem because he drank (old evangelism philosophy).
He drank, as any enlightened person knows, because he had a problem. Once his medical problem was cleared up, my friend quit drinking.
What damage would have occurred if I had tried first to correct his
drinking!

I bought a new dress shirt in a men's store early one morning. I was the
first customer of the day, and the clerk treated me rather rudely. He stuffed
the shirt into a bag, slammed my change on the counter, and gave me a few
choice words. I looked at him and said, "Buddy! Just because you had a big
fight with your wife this morning doesn't give you the right to talk to me
like that. You'd better get your act together before you ruin your business."

He backed up, laughed and said, "That's exactly what happened to me
this morning!" Symptoms indicate causes! People act like they do because
they are reacting to something else!

As a pastor I have become so convinced of this reality that it has
become almost impossible for anyone in our congregation to offend me.
If they are mad at me I just automatically assume they have a problem,
and I *know* it is not me! While this kind of attitude may be a little
simplistic it is at least comforting in its accuracy!

We do not have a problem because we do the negative things we do. We do
the negative things we do because we have a problem! In our proclamation,
dealing with today's sophisticated auditors, decisiveness is highly dependent on dealing with causal factors and not being overly preoccupied with
symptoms.

4. Do people understand my words?

The issue of semantics is always a critical concern to any devisive
proclamation. Am I just keeping the holy noise going, using all the right
buzz words in magnificent procession, or am I communicating? John
Wesley put the quandary this way, "Let but a pert, self insufficient animal,
who has neither sense nor grace, bawl out something about Christ, or his

blood, or justification by faith, and let his hearers say, 'What a fine gospel sermon'"!

We cannot logically expect to have a truly decisive ministry, or ever extend a meaningful invitation, if our words are not sound and true, thought out and pored over. As Albert Outler says, "The hearing of faith takes place in the context of the hearer's world view, not the preacher's" (*Theology in the Wesleyan Spirit*, p. 76).

My youngest son, who was only about four at the time, reminded me of this important truth one day. We were both at my office in downtown Miami late one afternoon when, leaving for home, I took a wrong turn and ended up on the crosstown expressway at 4:30! We were sitting in the world's longest parking lot. Cars sat eight lanes deep and stretched in both directions as far as the eye could see. Jimmy and I inched along in that quagmire with horns belching, tempers steaming, and radiators blowing, making little appreciable progress. After about ten minutes of starting and stopping, little Jimmy turned and said, "Daddy, why do they call this the "rush hour"?

Am I using words people understand? Are the words contemporary or at least meaningful. Are my words being delivered without the "holy whine" or Gothic verbosity? Am I contemporary? Am I attempting to pour my new wine into new wineskins or am I persisting in the presumptuous attitude of pouring old, old wine into new wineskins?

Much has been written about this hermeneutical need. I enjoy Lofton Hudson's book, *Grace Is Not a Blue Eyed Blonde!* This fascinating book explores precisely the crux of the problem of meaningful language, from the hearer's world view. Hudson encourages us to use words that are meaningful to us but also to be sure we are not using words for which the so-called "now" generation has no adequate orientation. "Grace" may mean something very religious and very precious to you, but to many of the folks listening to your message it conjures up visions of a beautiful blonde!

In *The Advocacy of the Gospel*, Lord Donald Soper gives us even better help in relating to today's culture. Dr. Soper points out that yesterday's congregation of the previous century heard what we had to say from the standpoint of knowledge of the Scriptures, a preoccupation with death, obvious guilt concerning their personal spiritual condition, and a sense of need. Soper says that today's auditor is no longer generally knowledge-able about faith, but must now hear words that instruct in the Scriptures and enable one to find faith. Soper also points out that today's auditor is no longer preoccupied with death but is interested in learning about how to live. Guilt, as a chief concern, has been replaced by doubt, and subtle curiosity has replaced a deep sense of need. How can I be decisive in ministry when my listeners do not know what I am talking about, and how can they know what I am talking about if I do not speak a language they can understand?

I personally struggle very hard with this concern. I want to be "contemporary," and yet I do not want to fall into undue compromise or into that lethal trap which says "oddity or even profanity grants instant contemporary."

In exploring this need for relevance, the old Youth for Christ slogan, "Anchored to the Rock but Geared to the Tide" has been of considerable help. If I would share a decisive proclamation I must stay close to the great truths but strive to ride the waves of my day.

Helmut Thielicke states this case in *The Trouble with the Church.* Thielicke writes, "The reference to the odor of decay that clings to the old, worn-out language applies only to the vocabulary which is simply passed on without being worked upon and digested, the vocabulary that shows no sign that it has gone through the medium of a living witness and is therefore brimful of associations with life that has been really experienced."

CONCRETION

If the proclamation is worth hearing, then it is worth acting upon. Life dictates this important principle in very simple terms: Ideas that fail to incite action tend to remain nebulous and then dissipate. Therefore, *concretion,* giving concrete commitment to my inspiration, is a logical conclusion to valid proclamation.

All of us, for instance, have heard a good story. We liked it and thought to ourselves, Surely I'll not forget that story. We did not write it down (give concretion to our inspiration). By the next day the story did not seem anywhere near as good as the day before, and by the following day we had forgotten it altogether! To be truly decisive there must be concrete expression.

I vividly recall the night I first knowingly encountered this principle. I was a senior in high school in Avon Park, Florida. I was a brand new Christian and had gone with others to a general time of "altar prayer" at the close of an evening service. After everyone else had returned to their seats, I simply could not leave the altar! Finally, my pastor came over and asked me if he could help me in any way. He also informed me that he was anxious to dismiss the congregation but could not do so as long as someone was still at the altar. I then reluctantly explained to him that I felt God was calling me into the ministry. After his initial surprise and delight he said, "Fine! What you need to do now is stand and tell the entire congregation!" I said, "No way!" He explained that I should, that it would help me. I explained that I didn't care what it did. I still wasn't going to stand up and tell anybody. Finally, after several minutes of slightly subdued arguing my pastor said, "Dean, you don't quite see the whole picture. There are two hundred people sitting out there watching you and me and waiting to go home. They will stay in their seats until I dismiss them, and I can stay here as long as you can!"

He literally made me get up and tell everyone what I felt I must do with my life. Then, I was bound to it! I had finalized my inspiration by *concrete* action. I specifically recall three distinct occasions in the remaining months of my senior year when I would have chucked the whole idea if I had not already told the whole world!

Concretion is part of the larger need for decisiveness. A soldier wears a uniform into battle to concretize his mission. There was a time, before the use of uniforms, when the same fighter was always found up on the ridge, no matter which army occupied it! They put a uniform on him (that is, formalized his inner commitment) and then he had to fight for someone and something.

This third dimension of decisiveness explains the evolution of marriage *in public*. Everyone who is married knows there comes a time in every marriage when you would not stay with it if you had not told the whole world where you stood and with whom you stood. Decisiveness dictates the principle of concretion. Invite them to put on the uniform! Invite them to get married in front of God and everybody!

Dietrich Bonhoeffer, in *The Cost of Discipleship*, puts the same truth this way, "Only he who is obedient believes, and only he who believes is obedient." Peter illustrates this commitment on the raging sea. As Christ approached, Peter had to put his foot out onto the sea. Zacchaeus, up in the tree, had to put his foot on the next lowest branch (concretize his inspiration). Levi had to get up and walk from behind the customs table in order to become Matthew.

Decisive evangelism is predicated on these three very important principles: If we hope to be a decisive, inspirational minister, we must first be as sure as we can of the *proclaimer*, who is saying these things. We must give critical attention to the *proclamation*, which is being said. And, we must be in touch with the expediency of *concretion*, formalizing our inspiration. Then, we are nearly ready to invite.

6. PERSPECTIVES AND ATTITUDES

For a mother to discover that *everyone's* five-year-old son acts like an unchained force of nature is a perspective worth forty boxcars of advice. In counseling, when persons feel like they are losing their minds, the perspective that this is a common and normal emotion for people struggling with life can be very uplifting and redeeming. To discover that everybody has moments where they feel lost smothers out many an unnecessary anxiety. This awareness and recognition, which allows you to get above it all for a more objective view, is called perspective.

Perspective is what I felt when a friend of mine mentioned how hard it was for him to go calling from door to door in his congregation. He said he often slipped silently into the driveway, closed his car door quietly, knocked timidly on the front door, left his calling card, and then, while driving carefully out onto the street, was constantly afraid someone would swing open the door and yell, "Yoo hoo, pastor, here I am!" I admire this man and his ministry very much. It helped greatly to discover that every minister has days of calling like that.

Let us observe our task of decisive ministry from one key perspective— What does my faith tell me about what God expects of me? What do the history, the tradition, and the heritage of my faith tell me about the bigger view of decisive ministry?

1. Practice what you preach.

I know from all those who have gone on before me that decisive ministry can be done if I have what I proclaim! This point is redundant from the previous chapter, but it should be treated here with dispatch: "I can't anymore give what I ain't got than I can come back from where I ain't been!"

We are describing "ethos." Ethos is corroborating evidence that supports what I am saying (ethic). Or, unless we live what we talk, there will never be decisive ministry! It is the same perspective Jesus taught when he *preached* on prayer (ethic) and "went to the Mount of Olives to pray as was his custom" (ethos).

The first perspective we need is to remember that God expects us to possess what we profess.

41

2. Try again.

I can do this kind of work if I remember that God expects me to attempt, to try, to be willing to fail.

It's like that story of Peter in the Garden at the betrayal. Do something! Don't just sit there! At least cut off somebody's ear—God can do more with our committed foolishness than he can with our perfect apathy. God expects to be given a chance to show divine power, and, therefore, God expects us to at least *try something!*

A member of my staff at Riverside Church, Miami, came into the office one day and stated the problem quite succinctly. Slumping into a brown leather chair in the corner of my office he looked at me for a moment and then said, "I've decided I need to make more mistakes around here!" I listened. "My main criticism of myself is that I've become too cautious. I'm doing everything "right" and nothing's happening!" He rose to his feet, walked to the door, and said, "Be prepared, Dean. I'm going to start making more mistakes!"

He did not know it, but as he spoke, he had just saved his job. More important, he had saved his job because he had brought himself back to a fundamental issue of decisive ministry. Our history and heritage remind us that God wants us to attempt, to try, to be willing to fail.

This perspective is imperative in almost any field of endeavor. I first began learning it when I was studying percussion instruments at The University of Miami during the summers of my high school years. One morning, while the concert band was playing one of Tchaikovsky's ponderous and heavily percussioned overtures, I was assigned to the snare drum and was busy trying to follow the score while not making any clearly distinguishable mistakes. Suddenly I was astonished to see the head percussion instructor come roaring through the band headed straight for me. I shall never forget what he said (or shouted) to me. "Martin!" He yelled, "You will never learn to play that, or any other instrument, or do anything else worthwhile, until you are willing to make big mistakes. The next mistake you make I want it heard all over campus!" The next mistake I made was heard all over campus and I was on my way not only to learn to play the snare drum but to acquire an important perspective for life.

In recent years we have learned to call this "hands-on experience." You and I are not going to learn to do some things without performing the task, and doing something necessitates making some mistakes. We can minimize these mistakes where possible, especially when dealing with the minds and souls of people, but God expects us to act, and the record clearly shows God can do more with failure than with no human attempt at all!

This important perspective comes very close to the heart of our venture into decisive, invitational evangelism. Am I willing to fail? This unjustified concern causes many of us to forego extending an invitation of any kind because we find ourselves thinking, "What if nobody responds? How will that make *me* look?" God can do more with my failure than with my perfect apathy. Accept that and bring fun, anticipation, and freedom to your ministry!

3. Be consistent.

Theological consistency, between ideology and methodology, is a must.

One of the difficulties and frustrations with decisiveness across The United Methodist Church arises precisely at this point. The United Methodist Church has long prided itself in being a noncreedal church. That is, this denomination is more pluralistic, more inclined, in the words of Wesley, to "think and let think." This position has been both our strength and our glaring weakness. It has been our strength because pluralism is a beautiful and special thing. *Pluralism* is the difference between a great orchestra (woodwinds, strings, percussion, and brass) and an "orchestra" made up of only bass drums or only tubas or only piccolos. Precisely because we, as a church, have not been a historically definitive church, we have fallen victim to a phenomenon that today is playing havoc with our denomination's need for theological consistency between ideology and methodology.

Put another way, The United Methodist Church, by its very nature as a noncreedal communion, tends to be vulnerable to the predominant *creedal* influence of its special and diverse geographical areas! Though you may not have clearly tied it in with the problem our church is having with indecisive evangelism, you have noted, for instance, that The United Methodist Church in New England tends to be very congregational in its methodology. It is still talking John Wesley but is living Jonathan Edwards! Noncreedal churches, residing within the bounds of strong creedalism, tend to take on the predominant methodologies of the existing majority influence.

In Wisconsin and Minnesota, The United Methodist Church *tends* to be very Lutheran in its methodology. Ministers will often be found talking of public witness and congregational involvement but will, in practice, baptize infants in private ceremonies. Some are also given extra fees for these services just as are their local Lutheran counterparts. Let custom be whatever custom is acceptable. My point is that noncreedal churches *tend* to take on the dominant methodological characteristics of the predominant creedal communion within their geographical area.

In the Southeast where I serve, as in the Southwest, the predominant creedal influence is Southern Baptist. The United Methodist Church, completely surrounded and dominated by such a strong, vital, and creedal church, has imitated the methodology of this pervasive influence to the detriment of its own growth and future. The United Methodist Church, throughout the Southeast and Southwest, continues to talk Wesley (grace, free will, institution as caretaker) but acts Calvinistic (election and institution as the source of salvation).

Now, the problem is not that the Baptists are wrong and that by tying our "right" theology to their "wrong" methodology we have created a bungling and indecisive mechanism. Not at all! When the Baptists take their theology, a theology that has meant so very much to so very many, and marries it to Baptist methodology—Come forward and join the church—their ministry has veracity and theological consistency.

When Methodists, on the other hand, take our wonderful theology, a word that has meant much to many, and marry it to institutional recruitment, it simply does not fit! Something is wrong, and just about everybody in the congregation senses this except the proclaimer!

Or, putting this principle within the framework of practical application, if I live and serve in the South, am pastor of a United Methodist church, and I spend twenty-five minutes in the service on a basic Armenian or Wesleyan sermon, and then end with Calvinistic methodology—an invitation to Christian discipleship, or, Please come join the church—very little can be expected of such a marriage!

Mixing ideologies and methodologies tends to produce subliminal static that is not conducive to receptivity or response. A Southern Baptist service will usually proceed with a fine, but basically informal singing service, followed by a sound Calvinistic sermon, ending with a very Calvinistic invitation—Be baptized and unite with this church. People are aided in their response because the service is consistent from start to finish. The closing of the service, the all-important invitation now under study, is both logical and sequential.

However, in the United Methodist church down the street, the minister might be practicing a peculiar and lethal hybrid of Wesleyan theology and Calvinistic (or Lutheran, or congregational) methodology that is confusing, bewildering, and nonproductive!

An Armenian sermon, a Wesleyan message, with its openness to free response, personal understanding, and theological latitude is required to have a Wesleyan ending, one that flows logically from the sermon. If we are going to be Congregationists (United Church of Christ) then so be it. If we are to be Lutherans or Roman Catholics or Southern Baptists, then, God bless you. Do it! But, if we are to serve in a Methodist church, then for God's sake let's find out *who* we are and whose we are. Let us break with the subtle intimations of the large creedal influence in our specific geographical area and become consistent in our proclamation. We will quickly find we have a marvelous message to share consistently, and the very act of sharing it will fortify our new resolve, and dissipate our timid spirits, through much greater response and productivity.

4. God is with us.

Finally, in order to be decisive and invitational in our ministry, we need to know God expects us to know that he is with us in this calling.

The closing chapter of this book, Chapter Ten, will deal with this important perspective in greater detail. For now, be reminded that we are not in this alone. When we respond to the call of God "to make disciples of all," and we are obedient, we remember God is still taking moldy old bread and insufficient fish, blessing them, breaking them, and feeding multitudes.

As for now, let us simply get above the other barriers that bewilder our perspective, complicate our task, and otherwise render us unable or unwilling to be invitational. Be reminded that God does expect us to possess what we proclaim, does expect us to try, to be willing to make mistakes, does expect us to be consistent in our approach, and does expect to walk this marvelous way with us. There are attitudes that can help!

7. GUIDELINES FOR EXTENDING THE INVITATION

If you have ever had the experience of moving through the uncharted Everglades of South Florida, as I did in my teenage years, you will know the need for "target palms." The long expanse of sawgrass offers no direction or guidance for the canoe traveler, or the person on the air boat or "swamp buggy." One will usually sight a tall palm standing sentinel over a lonely island hammock in the far distance. Then, by zeroing in on that landmark, the explorer makes a way to the safety and beauty of the island.

Guidelines are like that. By checking our direction against them from time to time, we are enabled to steer a truer course through the morass of ambiguity and confused motivations that beset us.

Here are some of the guidelines we can use for invitational evangelism.

Do I Want Anything to Happen?

Much has been written of late concerning the need for the *congregation* to approach the worship service "expectantly." Much encouragement has been given the congregation, through lecture and pen, to prepare mentally and spiritually for what God could do or might do in the forthcoming service. This first guideline—Do I want anything to happen—is not for the congregation as much as it is for the proclaimer. As the preacher going into the service to share the message I have prayerfully and tenaciously planned, do I really want anything to happen today, to these people, to *us!*

Motives are never wholly pure. Therefore, what I really want to happen in the service is often fuzzy at best and garbled at worst. When I attempt to appraise my motivation, in order to get at my expectations, I find I almost always *begin* approaching the pulpit with a desire to impress people with *me*. Then, recognizing this, I try to move as quickly as possible to more worthwhile goals. As I do, I find what I want to happen in the service changing right along with the awareness of motivation.

Why do you preach? One man said to me, "I preach to kill twenty minutes of an hour's assignment. That's why I preach!" Another minister in Ohio once said to me, "I preach hoping nothing will happen because I wouldn't know what in the world to do with it if it did." Still another minister said, "I'm afraid to encourage encounter because if no one responded I'd look pretty silly."

We see again that the question "Do I want anything to happen?" is closely related to the deeper question "Why am I in the work? Why do I preach?" The pastor, for instance, who is afraid he or she will look silly is fundamentally preaching to look good and therefore, if he or she doesn't become embarrassed, "what might happen" has *already* happened.

Do I want anything to happen? The answer, the "target palm" that must be kept in sight if I am to reach firm ground, dictates an emphatic "Yes!" I am preaching, not for display but for response. I may be fearful (Billy Graham has called the occasion of the invitation the most frightening moment in life), but I am willing to be vulnerable, run some risks, feel uncomfortable and unsure. So, as I go into the service, as the proclaimer, I want to enter expectantly. I want God to move, to prod, to encourage, to cause an effect regarding the proclamation. Without pretension or predetermination on my part, I want life to be different in some area for as many as possible who worship with me on this occasion. I have a right to expect that. As Matthew reminds us (13:58), "And he did not do many mighty works there because of their unbelief."

Little or nothing will happen unless there is within the being of the worship leader an expectant faith. Without this prime ingredient, this indispensable guideline, we are left to be much like the little boy who used to knock on my back door when I was a student preacher in seminary. Inevitably each spring he would come to my door clutching a dirty, damp little sack in his hand. He would look up at me and say, "You don't want to buy no grapes do you?" My answer, fostered by his expectancy, was equally predictable, "No!"

When I go to the pulpit to make a sales pitch for the most important values in all of life, let me constantly ask myself: Am I just putting in my time, or just entertaining the troops, or do I really want something to happen, for God, in the lives of the worshiping congregation?

What Do I Want to Happen?

Do I want something to happen which I can *see?* Something that affirms me? Something that makes me feel successful? If these are the things I want to happen, then my theological understanding of meaningful discipleship is grossly inadequate and needs immediate revision.

In decisive, invitational evangelism one of us may be commissioned to break up fallow ground. We go in, encounter useless or nonproductive soil, and we turn it over and then may be on our way to another field. Someone comes along behind us, and, as Paul reminds us in First Corinthians 3, may plant seed in the ground which someone else may have turned over and prepared for planting. Still someone else may come along and water that seed or cultivate it, or perhaps dig from around it any destructive weeds that may be endangering it. Then, the bright and wonderful day comes when someone else may actually reap the harvest of this mutual, Spirit-led effort! Those persons who always expect to see the results of their efforts inevitably feel wasted or useless, or perhaps simply nonproductive. Those persons who conceive of their lives as part of God's divine mosaic know that if they do what they can, where they can, as they can, in faith, God will use their efforts, and they will be part of the fellowship of decisive, invitational evangelism. As Spurgeon once said, "God has not called me to be successful but to be faithful."

In the local church we observe this scenario many times. I encountered one of the most conspicuous examples of the need to be in touch with "mosaic theology" my first year as a staff member of the old Board of Evangelism of The Methodist Church. I was at the office one morning getting ready to leave for a speaking engagement at a church in Illinois. I left my office to walk down the hall and encountered another staff member. This particular person was one of our most capable people and had also done a preaching mission at the same church where I was headed the year before. As we approached each other, my friend stopped and said, "I see on your schedule that you are going to West Frankfort."

"Yes," I replied, "I'm leaving in the morning."

"I was there last year," he continued, "and nothing happened. Nobody came, absolutely nothing happened period!" Then, as he walked away he glanced back and said, "Martin, you'll be lucky if your plane falls on the way!"

The conversation bothered me a little, not because of the possibility of the plane falling but because this man usually had very exciting and productive missions. I found the whole thought a little disconcerting. Nevertheless, I went to West Frankfort and had a wonderful week. Everyone came, everything happened, the harvest was plentiful! Throughout the week I kept hearing people say such things as, "This has been bothering me for months," "This thought has been eating at me for a year." Or "Some time ago I began to struggle with this or that need." I realized finally that my colleague from Nashville had had a wonderfully successful mission in that church (breaking up fallow ground and planting innumerable seeds) and upon my return to the office I told him what an uninformed and unfortunate farmer he was.

When we raise the question, What do I want to happen?, the answer usually is that we want to see the harvest. And, that may not be our assignment. By thinking in such an uninformed way, we tend to walk away thinking nothing happened when perhaps, in the timing and care of the Spirit, everything that could happen at that point did happen!

Another very common problem we have with this second guideline is the tendency to expect uniformity of response. Though we know better, we think that the 40 or 400 or 1400 who are there are all coming from the same place, with the same needs and in need of the same response. Of course not.

We would be much better off to leave it to the Holy Spirit to "translate" and transpire according to individual needs. We state the problem here but will amplify the practical answer, what to do about the problem, in Chapter 9.

What *should* I wish would happen? Simply this: that as many specific individuals in the congregation, as is heavenly or earthly possible, have an honest confrontation with the premise of the morning proclamation. That they must say "yes," "no," or "maybe." What I want to happen is that they, or we, come to grips in some meaningful and significant way, with the plow, the seed dropped, the water sprinkled, or the harvest time presented for decisive action in this service of worship.

Do I want anything to happen? Yes! I want those of us who are worshiping to make what decisions we can and will, and I want us to go as deep as we might on this particular and specific worship occasion!

Is There a Logical Sequence?

We looked at this problem in Chapter 4 but mention it here because it is an indispensable guideline.

The late Dr. Ronald Sleeth formerly of Perkins School of Theology, Southern Methodist University, put the homiletic experience into this perspective. He said three important facets had to be considered in a meaningful proclamation and worship experience: thesis, purpose, and response sought. My thesis may be: "Salvation is the process of being saved from something to something through God's grace." My purpose in the sermon may be best realized by raising the question, Why am I preaching this sermon? This query deals with the motivational question studied in the first guideline. Am I trying to impress, rationalize, protect, dramatize, fill up twenty-five minutes, inform, instruct, inspire, guide, motivate, counsel, persuade, or market? The answer to the question is my purpose. Sleeth says, "The thesis is a statement of the major affirmation of the sermon, the purpose is the reason for making that affirmation. Response sought is deciding precisely how I can end the sermon so that the worshipers will have an opportunity to respond, in kind, if they so choose." In my words, the most important guideline for extending the invitation is whether there is logical sequence between what I am saying and the response I am encouraging. If I spend twenty-five minutes pushing Hoover vacuum cleaners, I don't want to end the session with a three-minute plea for my listeners to buy Hershey bars! If I work all week on a sermon highlighting the virtues of a Chevrolet truck, I do not want to confuse my auditors by suddenly asking them if they want to buy a Ford! If I spend my allotted time for the worship experience encouraging people to grow in their faith and become more committed in their faith experience, I do not want suddenly to invite them to join the church. The purpose and response sought are nonsequential. Most probably, the person who is already a church member is one who most needs this specific confrontation.

Decisive, invitational ministry must be predicated on logical sequence among thesis, purpose, and response sought.

Is There Clarity of Explanation?

People today, while so very hungry for loving confrontation and decisiveness, are nevertheless quite conscious, and rightly so, of manipulative evangelism. They remember the revival trap and the magnificent manipulations of a "less sophisticated" era. Consequently, if the proclaimer does not adequately and clearly explain the response sought, especially if the opportunity is different from the usual, or if preaching in a setting unfamiliar with his or her work, many nervous or concerned worshipers may miss one of the most important opportunities of their lives.

I learned from ministers far more capable than I that, if the closing is to be the least bit unusual or different, before I begin the sermon I explain thoroughly to the congregation how I want them to consider ending the worship experience together. Second, if the closing is truly sequential, I can usually illustrate the closing experience in the rationale of the sermon (thus further briefing the congregation). Then, when I finish the sermon I once again thoroughly explain the culminating moments of the service.

Am I Being Sensitive to Personal Response Thresholds?

Not only must people be left to say "yes," "no," or "maybe," they must also be left to be themselves, to begin where they are, and to respond as they can to the claim of God on their lives. In short, everyone has his or her own response threshold, just as each one of us has his or her own pain, pleasure, frustration, and gratification threshold.

For instance, some people, due to personality, or home, or church orientation respond very easily to a sequential and intelligible invitation. They have few if any hangups, or they have never been placed in some well-worn groove. Others must struggle and work at response or must do so in some predetermined, approved way. Because all of us come from different places we may need permission to enter different gates to the Kingdom!

This awareness of individual response thresholds is a particularly helpful target palm on the horizon in noncreedal churches. Noncreedal churches do not tend to have highly restricted, defined, and stereotypical invitations. In most pluralistic or noncreedal churches, the congregation has never encountered any inflexible models of surrender handed down generation to generation by God. As a result, given half a chance, they can and will respond to the invitation with simple and refreshing ease.

This great and important truth first began to dawn upon me when I went to Atlanta for seminary training at Emory University. I was assigned to a wonderful little middle Georgia community as student pastor. I immediately began trying to get people to "come to the altar." The people of my church were of the old aristocratic South and were simply incapable of responding in ways that were superficial to them. An altar call was not their response threshold. Plus they had no grounding in Second Great Awakening methodology!

One day, as I was agonizing in prayer over my "failure to harvest," it was as though God spoke to me outright. I distinctly felt these words, "Martin! Do you want to make these people like you or are you willing to allow them to be themselves before me?" The question stung deeply because I did want them to be like me. Such response would be flattering, affirming, reassuring, and "proof" of success. I was much like the man in R. Buckminister Fuller's tale who went overboard from a sinking ship and could not swim. As he flailed away in the water, a piano lid from the ship's saloon came floating by. The half-drowned man grabbed the lid, dog-paddled to the nearest island, and spent the rest of his years manufacturing piano lids for people drowning at sea! I, too, wanted these middle Georgia folks to do it like I did it!

After this startling experience, I approached the culmination of the service more sequentially and with more sensitivity, allowing people to respond as they could and as *God* directed them. Things began to happen because I had finally come to the place where I was allowing God's Spirit to work with individuals on individual levels.

Allowing for individual response thresholds is an important guideline. I once saw this critical target palm stated this way in one of E. Stanley Jones Ashram newsletters:

> No, it is not for *you* to open the buds into blossoms. Your touch soils them, you tear their petals to pieces and strew them in the dust; he who *can* open the bud does so so simply.

Since that important juncture in my unofficial seminary education, I have noticed, regarding varying response thresholds, that people accept good news in direct proportion to their basic personality. If you are the type, for instance, who would jump up and down and shout for joy if someone unexpectedly gave you a million dollars, then that's precisely how you would act upon reception of the greatest Good News of all! If, on the other hand, you simply lowered your head, upon the announcement that you had been given a million dollars, and said, "Isn't that wonderful? I sure don't deserve it, but I sure am grateful," then that is precisely the way you will respond to the Good News of God in Christ. We must all be ourselves in expressing our faith and in responding to faith.

As I keep the guidelines before me to help me become a decisive inviter, I must surely remember that people are coming from different places and, therefore, must enter at different gates. I must not ask one person to be yet another person. I must allow persons to respond where they are, as they are, according to their need and ability to deal with their needs.

When people are allowed to come through the door which is truly theirs, the predictable downer following the commitment is not as drastic or dramatic. They have not been artificially induced to climb up twenty feet to sail off into their new life of faith when, in fact, they simply needed to step over a slight rise in the floor. As a result, they will not be required to face as much postadrenaline depression, the downer, the "that sure didn't last long" syndrome, as will be faced by those unnaturally pushed beyond their natural response threshold.

When we attempt to deal with the need of people to respond to God's will and way for their life, we are, at best, in a lonely sawgrass wilderness. No persons would undertake such a pretentious and precarious occupation unless they were either fools and knew no better or called of God and had no choice. If we are called of God and have no choice, then we need to be about the business of decisive evangelism. We need to extend to people an invitation to do something about the proclamation of the hour. In doing this we need at least these important guidelines:

- Do I want anything to happen?
- What do I want to happen?
- Is there logical sequence?
- Is there clarity of explanation?
- Am I sensitive to response thresholds?

8. HELPING THOSE WHO DO RESPOND

People need informed assistance, and the fact that so many of us do not know what to do is possibly the chief inhibition from extending invitations.

Many of us in noncreedal churches are like the minister I know who said to me, "I wouldn't know what to do or say if someone should respond to my invitation." Or, we are afraid of being caught in the bind of the Ohio minister who once told me that, shortly after his own conversation, he extended his first public invitation. This particular invitation, sequential to the message, asked for a public acknowledgment of surrender or commitment. When the invitation was given, a man came forward obviously moved, according to my friend, and deeply in earnest about the condition of his life. My friend walked down from the chancel, shook his hand, talked with him about the weather, and invited him to return to his seat. As this inquirer passed through the front door after the hymn he said, "Pastor, I still need help." The pastor replied, "I know you do, and so do I. I'll find out what I can and get back to you." Some of us are hesitant to extend invitations because we would not know what to do if anyone did respond. Still others react with misplaced hostility. Yet others cover up with quasi-indifference. Others overcompensate and move into the safe haven of polarity by asserting nonthinking, insensitive mandates.

Like the congregation itself, we the proclaimers also come from different places, manifesting different needs, epitomizing varying compassions and concerns. But, whatever our background or orientation each one of us looks at the "holy moment" with one thing in common: fear, that is, awe. If the desire to run away and hide is not lurking somewhere in the conscious or unconscious mind, then the proclaimer probably does not understand the gravity of the situation.

Let us make an honest attempt to find practical help in the awesome responsibility of assisting the inquirer. Let us look at the subject under three basic headings: (1) problems and misconceptions facing the inquirer, (2) difficulties to be faced by the counselor, and (3) possible approaches.

Problems and Misconceptions
Facing the Inquirer

When a person comes forward at the end of a service, or enters my office during the week, or comes by my home in the evening—whenever and wherever he or she may choose to accept my invitation to respond to my message—I must never naively assume that everything is as it appears on the surface. This is not just a simple human being facing a moment of truth with God. This is a complex person struggling with, or maybe against, fears or preconceptions that may be rooted in the present or, as often as not, may go back deep into early childhood. Deep childhood bruises may be rendering this person incapable of believing in a loving, forgiving God. Present complexities may find expression in fear of what this surrender may mean to one's lifestyle or future plans. The individual may simply be concerned, as many are, about the question, will I be able to live this commitment?

Inquirers come with a bedeviled mixture of motives and wandering motivations. They come not only needing help right now but also having needed help long before this particular confronting invitation. They come to me as pastor, not needing an amateur psychiatrist who can help "reassimilate a personality." They come needing the assistance of a friend who will help them gingerly or courageously cross the bridge of faith in Christ. I must be this friend, but it will help me in the task to realize some of the more common problems and misconceptions which are brought to this holy moment.

Many people come toward faith with a very poor image or understanding of the true nature of God. It is not information they have, but misinformation. It is not conception but misconception. If this is true, they will need help in the response to the invitation because their childhood image of God, derived from parental models in childhood, is inadequate if not destructive. Persons, for instance, who have never had anyone in their lives whom they could trust, will find it most difficult to "trust" God. Others of us have never really been loved. Others of us grew up in homes where forgiveness for anything was hard to come by, or virtually nonexistent. Perhaps our inquirer is oriented toward a concept of God which J. B. Phillips refers to in his marvelous little book *Your God Is too Small* as "the resident policeman." Many people I talk with about a personal faith have yet another imagery problem. They were raised to be so fearful of making mistakes—getting "blasted" if they did—that they are very reluctant to enter into a relationship with yet another "Parent" who may not give them a fair chance to attempt, fail, learn, and then attempt again. Still others may have trouble responding to deeper commitment because they were raised in a home where nothing was expected of them. They were, are, and always will be perfect in the eyes of their parents, and they have no capacity to understand the need for change.

In personal counseling in my office, at the chancel rail, or at general prayer time in the pews following the message, I have found it extremely helpful to be aware of the part which early childhood orientations play in the conscious or subconscious mind of the inquirer. Often a person can be helped to accept the real God of the universe while forever, and for good reason, they may remain unable to respond to the god of their childhood, environmental, or sociological orientations.

The minister who would be decisive and invitational should get in touch with this dynamic. I found great help in this area from J. B. Phillips' book and also from Hugh Missildine's two excellent books, *Your Inner Child of the Past* and *Your Inner Conflicts—How to Solve Them* (Simon and Schuster).

Another very real problem brought to the moment of counseling concerns the misconceptions surrounding the imagery of conversion itself. I often encourage individuals to read E. Stanley Jones' book *Conversion* for help with their imagery. All of us have images of how "it" happens, what will happen, how we will feel, and so on. Simply if not simplistically stated, most misconceptions in imagery surrounding the time of surrender (or precisely *how* we think we *must* respond to an evangelistic invitation *if* it is to be *authentic*) can be traced to how "my brother did it," or my mom, or Uncle John or Aunt Clarabell, and so on. Thus, driven by our inner preconceptions, if not pressured by overt representatives of specific piano lids, we shuffle off into the unknown, or more often than not, refuse to shuffle, because "they" are really not "us," and no one has yet informed us that we do not have to have identical experiences.

Yet another point of assistance often needed by the inquirer, and another important argument for sequential invitations, is help in isolating specifically that which she wants God to do in or for her life. The nature of the two previous disorientations, the inquirer's understanding of both God and conversion, often makes it very difficult for him to know what he needs and, in times like this, a caring and objective friend can be of immeasurable help. Not only must the person wanting to respond to the invitation be helped to isolate her specific need, she must also be helped to make a clear decision as to whether or not she is really looking for a deeper life. The motives of the seeker can be just as untested and disruptive as can be that of the proclaimer.

For instance, many times the response of the inquirer will actually be as "conscience sop." We want "something" to happen to us that will help us "not feel quite so bad or guilty." Christian conversion, the most important and highest form of evangelistic inviting, certainly possesses the important ingredient of peace and well-being, but "feeling better" may not be the true aim of the sermon shared. In reality, feeling better would be but the *by-product* of surrendering one's life to Christ. Or, as Cannon Byron Green of Great Britain once said, many inquirers also need help because "they seek a 'blessing' instead of the Blesser."

One should indeed expect a sense of joy in forgiveness, but it is sheer folly to seek the product instead of the Producer. The counselor may need to stand ready to help the inquirer understand that the Producer will bring the product along. The one who has responded to my invitation may need to hear the words, "Seek ye *first* the kingdom of God, and *his righteousness,* and these other things will be added unto you."

Commensurate with this awareness, many inquirers of our generation are called the "now" generation. We call them the Yuppie generation (young, upwardly mobile professionals) because every time anything new comes along and someone asks, "Do you need this?" their first and immediate answer is, "Yup!"

We are constantly seeing people in our congregations who have gone after all there is to get but are now asking, "Isn't there more? This doesn't make it! There's got to be something else!" Consequently, they do not come toward faith because they need to be *obedient* to the cross of Christ but because they want what Christ can do for them. They want an immediate and satisfying walk in the rose garden of faith. And, of course, ours is not the first generation to mistake God for the gardener (John 20:15). But our generation is the group to whom we proclaim the eternal truths of God and, as the proclaimer, I need to help inquirers understand precisely what it is they are after. Do they want the product or the Producer? In this clarifying role I can help inquirers appreciate that the new life in Christ will have its great moments of joy and unspeakable beauty.

Still other seekers are looking for deliverance from various hells of all descriptions, sizes, and expressions, here or eternally. Yet other people are inadvertently seeking greater conformity with their Western culture. Whatever it is we seek, we are not apt to find it until we do two things: (1) realize that what we are seeking is not what we ought to be seeking and (2) zero in on what it is we really should be after. Some people call it "intentionality." Wesley put it this way: "We must be singular or be damned." Most of us remember this important insight from the early teen years when we walked into our closets, declared our favorite shirt was nowhere to be found, only to have our mother walk in and put her hand on it immediately! Our feeble response was, "Well, it wasn't there when I looked!" Mom was deliberate and we were dallying. One of the problems or misconceptions facing the inquirer is the need to be intentional, or at the very least, have someone help them find this important key: the need to be deliberate.

As you might remember from your own experience, another area where the inquirer gets derailed is over the general subject and meaning of the word *surrender*. Surrendering to someone or something is a very intimidating concept for many people. This is particularly true of people who have made previous surrenders and have been badly burned. Integrity in surrender is a scary thought for most of us. Unconditional surrender is the key to any relationship.

Another of E. Stanley Jones' books, *Victory Through Surrender*, contains much practical and significant advice concerning the need to understand better and explain surrender. In this book Dr. Jones explores the logic of surrender. He explores it as a paradox to our understandings of reality, and he helps us see that no person either fully accepts, or is fully accepted, unless she or he gives all. Dr. Jones points out, when we finally give our all, we then find the greatest freedom, the freedom to receive God's all.

Another misconception that often comes with the seeker to the moment of truth is the rampant misconception of our day that usually finds expression in one of two forms: (a) that one must earn salvation, that I am not "worthy" and decidedly "not deserving." The seeker should be directed to the fundamental tenet of Ephesians (2:8), "by grace you have been saved through faith: and this is not your own doing, it is the gift of God." Or, (b) the very opposite position, namely, that *nothing* is required. Here the counselor may need to expose the seeker to such words as *surrender, restitution* (a very important word so often overlooked in contemporary evangelical theology), *resolution*, or perhaps just the simple word *discipline*. In both (a) and (b), people often need help in distinguishing between "earning" and "working." We do not earn our way in, but the fruit of our belonging is the work we do for others.

Many people fail to realize the forgiveness of God because they cannot bring themselves to forgive themselves! God has forgiven them. The grace of God has been operative in their lives. They have been responsive to God through faith, but they fail to appreciate this reality because they sustain a subconscious desire to "make amends" by self-flagellation. It is a common, fruitless endeavor. These people must be helped to see that they are not more pious or righteous than God. If God can forgive them, they ought to be able to forgive themselves and not waste precious energy on self-punishment.

These are a few of the primary problems and misconceptions brought by all of us to the point of encounter with God. This list is not inclusive but does pinpoint the most evident and persistent among our preconceptions, poor orientations, and superficial emotional baggage.

Difficulties to Be Faced by the Counselor

Earlier in this chapter I mentioned the one common ingredient, fear (awe), which lurks in everyone assisting people in their exploration of faith. The counselor must recognize and appreciate the universality of fear as it relates to any tremendously important task. Like the soldier, the surgeon, the marriage counselor, or the air traffic controller, to understand your critical task is to expect and even appreciate this predictable element. Those persons who are fortunate enough to have a job that is critical and exacting, must learn to live with fear. They find it invigorating, enlivening, stimulating, and important to peak performance. No task is more important or more critical than the ministry of invitation. Thank God for it. Accept and utilize the emotions that come with it!

If, as someone has said, "courage is fear that has said its prayers" and, if productive people involved in important work must live beyond what brings comfort, we need to consider what it means to be a *channel* of God's grace.

Unfortunately we often see ourselves as "the one" who has got to "produce." We busy ourselves learning "how to win people to Christ," getting the right technique down to a fine art. We concern ourselves with results. Again, Spurgeon had it right, "God has not called me to be successful but to be faithful."

We are channels of grace, not grace itself. God does not need us for techniques, but God does need us as a thoroughfare! God wants to move through our lives to bring Truth to light in other persons' lives according to their need, their willingness, their understanding.

In the early days of my ministry, as I tried to learn how to "win people" to Christ, I read a little book entitled *Soul Winning*. The book instructs the reader on how to "get" the person. It teaches how to systematically manipulate persons into "decision," how to get them to "do the right thing." I quickly learned, thank God, that "winning" a person is not the point! The task of the inviter is being a loving and caring channel for God to touch someone's life. I appreciate the thought from Paul found in the dedication of this book (2 Cor. 4:1,2, The Living Bible): "It is God himself, in his mercy, who has given us this wonderful work, and so we never give up. We do not try to trick people into believing—We are not interested in fooling anyone. All such shameful methods we forego." I, as the inviter, must regularly be reminded that I am not the champion of God in the world, rather, I am God's channel to the world.

Many counselors still face the difficult task of assuming responsibility for winning people. I believe this is a harmful position both for the counselor and to the seeker. To deal with this, I must constantly and consciously remind myself that (a) God is much more willing to help this person than I; (b) God knows better how to reach the individual than I ever shall; and (c) these two principles can be brought together only as God has open and willing channels available to use.

Counselors, or the inviter, must also be conscious of yet a third area of personal difficulty: wanting people to start from where the counselor feels they ought to be.

My family and I have done much camping over the years. We have thoroughly enjoyed hooking up our trailer and heading for woods, open sky, peace and quiet. One thing I learned was that no matter how much you may want that trailer to go with you, no matter how sincere you are in your desire, no matter how well you may drive your car, you have to back all the way to where the trailer is to get it hooked up. Helping people in their inquiry after God is very much the same.

We cannot hook up with people and take them with us on a great journey if we do not go where they are and hook up where they live. That is, we dare not assume that everyone is like the last person we were privileged to help, or that "they should know more" about theology or faith than they do, or that they ought to be further down the road of Christian understanding, or that they are not ready, or whatever. Be sure to start with them where they are, and not where you are, or think they ought to be.

Similar to this difficulty is another problem area, not so much for the inquirer but for the inviter: the tendency to overfeed. People can digest only so much. Therefore, the counselor must be careful not to demonstrate her own profound knowledge of faith. She must carefully and prayerfully give to the seeker that which will nourish his need *for now* and thus can be assimilated without causing him to strangle. Or, as Paul reminds us in First Corinthians, give them the sincere milk of the Word and not strong meat, for now.

Another great difficulty facing most counselors for those people acting in response to invitation is developing the fine art of listening. I often find it most difficult to actually listen to people because I am anxiously looking for an opening to pour in profound utterances and clever sayings. Listening in a caring framework is mandatory. In his wonderful book, *Ask Me to Dance*, Bruce Larson relates Paul Tournier's philosophy concerning this need. Dr. Tournier felt that people had misunderstood Jesus when he talked about being fishers of men. "After all," he said, "no one wants to be caught by somebody else. So I sit by the bank without a fishing pole in my hand and enjoy the scenery. Fish seem to sense that I'm not trying to catch them. They come to me just to talk about themselves and about life. Then from time to time, some do get caught by Jesus Christ, and I am more surprised than they are."

Finally, be available! Harried people cannot relate to hurried people!

Joseph Bayly has written a fascinating little book entitled *The Gospel Blimp*. It is the story of some well-intentioned Christians who want to reach one particular man for Christ. Their main strategy rests in the purchasing of a big blimp, the Gospel Blimp. They finally raise enough money to buy the thing, and then they begin hovering over the victim's house, dropping gospel tracts and calling out scripture verses through an overly loud amplification system. One day, however, the targeted neighbor comes over in deep distress to ask for help from one of the main blimp operators. The blimp leader dismisses the victim because he must hurry down to the hangar for a committee meeting to discuss planting flowers and shrubbery around the blimp hangar. After all, the blimp man reasons, how can we "reach" anyone if we continue to fly our blimp out of a hangar area that is not properly landscaped? The golden opportunity to reach the man is missed all because no one had time to do the very thing they were supposed to be doing!

This marvelously irritating story reminds us, the Gospel Blimp operatives, that we must constantly reassess our priorities and put *people* first. Everything else, except the man standing at your door asking for or needing your time, is daisy planting. Be available!

The invitational counselor does bring these and other difficulties to the moments and days after the sermon. Each of the skills gained from other sources of counseling can be brought to your invitational preaching. Here we can remember one important rule. God can do more with our committed failure than with our uncommitted perfection. Therefore, let us take our bumps and blemishes out into the world, and let God use us.

Let us live beyond our comfort zone and be a channel through which God can pour out love and grace to a needy world.

Possible Approaches

I write this section because I meet ministers all across America who need some *specific* reference point for further evaluation and assessment of this important and practical subject. My hesitation in suggesting possible approaches is based on concern over my lack of knowledge, the desire not to perpetuate manipulative methodology, and a fear of oversimplification. However, my motivation to include it is much simpler and much stronger. Many of us want help at this point regardless of inherent pitfalls. Most of us have enough sense to use suggestions rather than allow suggestions to use us.

Take a look at some possibilities for approaching people who are making inquiry based on an invitational sermon. The following suggestions are primarily oriented toward someone who may be seeking a personal conversion experience. While invitation, if truly sequential to the message, could be an open door for any decision, one subject must serve as an example. Nothing is more important in ministry than extending the decision to accept Christ.

1. Ask inquirers why they have come and what they want God to do in their lives. After they have dug as deeply as they can, give them time to pray in their own words concerning their need.

2. A second but more hazardous approach is to help the inquirer "word a prayer." I mention this because in this day of an incredible lack of knowledge about God, what someone else has called "ignosticism," I am finding more and more people who want to pray but simply do not "know the right words." I can spend a lot of time lecturing them on the fact that there are no "right" words, or I can spend a little time helping them word their prayer.

The hazards of putting words into a person's mouth can be greatly reduced by prayerfully listening and caring. After you spend some time with the individual, in a listening and caring attitude, you should be able to assist that person in putting the essence of his/her concern into words.

Often, for instance, in a guest for conversion, I will ask the person responding to my invitation to "pray the following prayer," or "use your own words along the following line." The prayer is often as follows (pausing between sentences for them to repeat or reword): "Dear God, I do not pretend to understand all that I am doing. I do not come claiming to be deserving, or pretending to be worthy. You know I have a long way to go and need your help in getting there. Right now, therefore, as an act of simple faith, I confess my failures before you and, in an act of intelligent worship, I do receive Jesus Christ as my personal Savior and Lord. With faith I thank you! Amen."

A worded prayer, whatever the subject of surrender, after much listening and caring, can be very helpful to many people.

3. Another option is to show inquirers a verse from the Bible relating to their quest; for example, 1 John 1:9: "if we confess our sins he is faithful and just to forgive us and cleanse us from all unrighteousness." This "written guarantee" can be of real help to many people. Then, help them appreciate the integrity of God. God offered forgiveness! God's promise will not be broken.

4. If it is "feeling" they are after, and are making no headway because they cannot feel God's presence, encourage them to truly "take God at his word," to accept love and forgiveness by faith. Encourage them to contract with God. That is, encourage them to lay their lives in God's hands and consider the transaction (of faith) done. I have seen many who walked away in faith walk ultimately, in due time and season, into feeling and assurance. But, it is imperative to help them understand that the starting point is not feeling but faith! Seek *first* the kingdom of God, and God's righteousness, and all other things will come as they may!

5. Be sure to give inquirers practical guidance concerning the next few days. Help them understand that what goes up must come down, and faith feelings or emotions are not exceptions to that rule. If they do experience high feelings of assurance, peace, or ecstasy, they must count on counterbalancing moments of emotional recovery (again, called post-adrenaline depression). Help them appreciate both the normality and the necessity of this kind of healthy emotional maintenance.

Help them appreciate and be prepared for doubts, temptations, and low moments that would be predictable in any new undertaking. Encourage them to become involved in private prayer, prayer groups, corporate worship, and Bible study. Help them to appreciate the need to develop and maintain personal devotional habits and public involvement in Christian fellowship. Help them understand the importance of good habits and healthy discipline as vital aids to a growing and healthy faith.

6. Where you can, give them personal follow-up in their new decision. Visit them in the early days following their choice, especially in the case of newborn infants in Christ. Encourage them. Pray with and for them.

Now that we have taken a close look at the subject of how to be a practical help to those making inquiry into a personal faith, let us move over to the sanctuary. Let us explore *examples*, not infallible methods or guaranteed models, that may offer someone a real chance to respond positively to your decisive invitation.

9. EXAMPLES FROM ALL OVER

During the years I served with the staff of The Board of Discipleship of The United Methodist Church I made careful notes on forms and variations of decisive evangelism which I observed throughout the church. Some of the models reported are foreign to my temperament. I personally would be very uncomfortable with announcing some of these invitations. Others, which are special to me, may not fit your approach at all. Some of these models may incite your interest. Others will serve to stimulate new approachers to invitation in your preaching. Still other invitations may leave you wondering how God could possibly put up with all of our diversity!

Someone once pointed out to me that a simple measure for the validity of an invitation (other than being decisive and sequential) is your attitude: If you think it will assist people in their own decisiveness, then it probably will!

1. **Each proclaimer should have a basic M.O. (mode of operation).** Each preacher must discover what is for him or her a specific model of invitation that can be used most Sunday mornings. It is superficial and probably a gimmick to expect the preacher to arrive at the close of every Sunday morning service with a new, novel, and totally original approach to decisiveness. Each minister should find what model of invitation fits his or her preaching style but allows for opportunities of decisiveness. This model will be employed most of the time.

2. **The speaker should develop a sensitivity to logical complimentation.** That is, on special Sundays, or with special subjects, there will be an invitation that is different from your standard M.O. This variation may offer a much better chance for sequential response to your special message or occasion. This special change of pace for the invitation will also flow logically and sequentially from the context of the proclamation and must fit that special message like a glove. These occasional deviations from the norm may also serve to prompt further creativity as well as offer life, longevity, and resilience to your standard sermon style. Many of the following examples will illustrate possibilities for such a change of pace in extending the invitation.

65

In these examples you may find your own standard style, if you have not already done so. In the other examples you may find two or three that will give you a new approach for decisive moments following the sermon where your standard M.O. needs a rest.

EXAMPLE 1: GROUP COUNSELING

I begin with the one invitation that is my own standard workhorse. Like most good standards it lends itself to earnest and honest prayer concerning the subject of the morning. I call this example of decisive invitation "group counseling." I use it at the end of nearly every sermon I share.

At the close of the service I ask the congregation to bow their heads and make their pew an altar of prayer. I ask them to consider prayerfully the key idea of the message of the service, which might be conversion, social responsibility, stewardship, or being more loving. I then give them adequate time on their own to deal with the subject, as they can and if they will, during private, individual prayer. On many occasions, for those who want to respond but do not know "the right words," I slowly word a prayer that might assist them in making a meaningful commitment concerning this subject.

I make a strong effort to place myself in the same frame of mind as if I were kneeling at the altar rail with an individual and he/she was saying, "Pastor, I want to act on this proposition, but I don't know how to pray." In a personalized case like that, I would help the individual word an appropriate prayer. And, I have learned that most of our people do not know how to pray specifically concerning specific personal needs. I therefore respond to their earnest quest with care not to manipulate, by giving them practical help. I also often add, "If you are here and do not have the courage to respond to this message, or are simply not ready, or are just not interested, then you are invited to remain courteous and patient. No one is going to manipulate you here. The service will be dismissed shortly." This simple and occasional addition to our "group counseling" time can convey many meaningful things to people throughout the congregation.

The obvious results of this model continue to strengthen my faith day by day. Evidence of genuine response and transformed lives accumulates over the years. This is my standard M.O. You may be comfortable with this, have your own, or find your basic approach somewhere else. A minister in California often invites people to come and go from the chancel during the singing of the closing hymn. He has a large church, but the people move freely in this act of worship. And, for many of them, the moment is very decisive. Another similar derivation is to invite people during the closing hymn to remain for altar prayer after the benediction. After the hymn the minister goes to the altar for a moment of prayer alone. He then remains in case others want someone to pray with them. Once you identify your general approach, you will discover a freedom and an excitement in proclamation ministry that can only come from regular and intelligent involvement in decisive evangelism.

EXAMPLE 2: WRITTEN RESPONSE

A minister in Wisconsin once told me of his sermon, "Do You Know Which Nail Is Sticking Through Your Shoe?" His premise was the necessity of identifying the irritating or destructive intrusion and then dealing with it. At the conclusion of the sermon he invited the congregation to take the blank 3" x 5" card provided for them in the back of the pew and write down their greatest hurt (or most earnest prayer, etc.). He then invited those who wished to take a moment to pray at the altar and leave their card as a symbolic gesture of placing the problem in God's hand.

On another occasion the same minister used the identical invitation but had the cards passed down the pew to ushers who brought them forward to be presented, as a group, for prayer. This model was thematic and sequential. According to the pastor it presented a marvelous opportunity for decisive worship on that particular Sunday morning. With all of those unsigned cards, he said, "I held in my hands a virtual gold mine of information on what my people were really thinking, needing, and feeling."

EXAMPLE 3: QUIET TIME

A common invitation to decisiveness used throughout the country is the quiet time of general altar prayer. In this example the congregation is invited to approach the altar at the close of the service and return to their seats when they are ready to do so. Many ministers use this particular model as their standard M.O.

Another pastor once told me of a model that is a combination of examples 1 and 3. From time to time he invites people to pray silently in their seats. Then, as they have finished praying about the subject of the morning they are asked to stand. After everyone is standing, the pastor then dismisses the service.

EXAMPLE 4: STAND AND COMMIT

Another minister when preaching on personal surrender to Christ or any subject related to renewal or reconciliation, asks those who have responded during that service to stand following the message. He had, on one occasion, preached on how important it is to give physical acknowledgment to inner commitment. He explained that this is why we get married in public, why a soldier salutes and wears a uniform, etc. Logically, in this setting, he said to the congregation, "This morning, if you stand you are saying, 'I open my heart to Christ and accept his forgiveness. This is my witness to my surrender. Please pray for me.'"

A pastor in Australia will occasionally close the service by selecting a hymn that reiterates the basis of the morning message. He then asks the people to remain seated while the hymn is sung. He also instructs them to stand, individually, only when they come to that part of the hymn that tickles their inner commitment of the morning. For instance, he often uses "Just as I Am," and some people stand at "just as I am." Still others stand at "though tossed about." Others stand at "with many a conflict, many a doubt," and so on. He has found this expression a meaningful and occasional expression of decisiveness.

EXAMPLE 5: NOTICE OF AVAILABILITY

A very competent young pastor, one time out of every four or five worship experiences, offers a "Notice of Availability." He says, "After the service, if you want to hear more about the subject of the morning, or respond to it in any way, I will be over in the chapel (or room so and so) following the closing hymn." This simple expression of availability gives significant opportunity for people to respond to this preacher's invitation of the morning.

EXAMPLE 6: COMMUNION COMMITMENT

On the first Sunday of the month, Holy Communion is celebrated in a Florida church. The minister, using a contemporary ritual to the Communion, places the actual coming to the altar for communion before the message. The message follows on the subject "Where Do We Go From Here?" How do you grow in this commitment? The congregation is then dismissed and encouraged to go out and give concrete evidence to their commitment "to walk from henceforth in God's holy way."

One minister regularly uses the Communion Sunday as an "invitation" affording respite and resilience to her standard M.O. She customarily uses Communion Sunday to speak on Christian conversion, the new birth, surrender, the doctrine of salvation by faith, and so on. Then, logically, having explained the real meaning of the elements involved in the service, she explains to the people how they can come to the communion rail and participate through receptive faith, "Ye that do truly and earnestly repent of your sins." She makes a regular and meaningful invitation out of the communion service.

Dr. Larry Lacour, presently professor of preaching in the seminary at Oral Roberts University is, in my opinion, one of the church's leaders in the field of meaningful, nonmanipulative, and yet decisive ministry. Larry uses the Communion service *every Sunday* as a decisive opportunity. Some liturgists may not approve of his atmosphere for Communion, but one senses a healing and sensitive approach which keeps the walk-in Communion from feeling like a sacramental assembly line.

My experience in the Navy taught me the importance of Holy Communion at each Sunday morning service. In divine worship, we had Disciples of Christ, Episcopalians, Roman Catholics, Lutherans, and others who felt they had not worshiped without the sacrament. As a pastor I found these backgrounds also in church members. So in Colorado Springs we announced in the bulletin that the sacrament would be served in the adjoining chapel immediately after the 10:55 service. Often I made a special appeal in the sermon and indicated that I, personally, would meet with those who came for communion.

Our most effective use of the sacrament happened Maundy Thursday. On that day, we scheduled "walk-in" communion from eight in the morning until eight in the evening. In the chapel, of course, continuous recorded organ music played throughout the twelve hours. Upon arriving to commune, persons would be seated and encouraged to pick up a bulletin which carried the communion ritual with the suggestion that when they were ready to commune they should come forward and the minister would serve them. I found this one of the most meaningful ministries of the year. As individuals, couples, or families would come forward and kneel, I would kneel on the other side and ask such questions as, "Is there something special on your heart that you would like to talk or pray about before you commune?" So often they would share, many times in tears. The combining of counselling and prayer before communing is a very personal means of grace. When three professors started St. James United Methodist Church in Tulsa, one of the first actions of the congregation was to vote that we have Holy Communion every Sunday morning. As a result I would use the sacrament, adapting the conclusion of my sermon, to make communing an appropriate response to the sermon. Any who wished special prayer or counsel could raise a hand as they knelt, and one of us would minister to them specifically. This, too, proved to be greatly used and became a means of grace.

EXAMPLE 7: RESPONSE GUIDE

A Response Guide is a paper containing a clear rationale for decisiveness and a page or two with four different categories for possible response. The categories are: My Relationship to God, the Church, Other People, and Myself. Under these subtitles are a number of possible commitments that can be checked off, if the worshiper so chooses as his or her response to the morning message. The actual checking is designed to help the worshiper thoroughly think through options and possibilities for deeper commitment in these four vital areas of life. Sometimes the guide is brought to the altar by ushers or during general altar prayer by the congregation. Sometimes they are simply left on the pew following a dedicatory prayer and the benediction.

EXAMPLE 8: GENERAL ALTAR CALL

A pastor in Minnesota uses an old-fashioned altar call with great effectiveness. He knows there are many people, as in all denominations, who are not only oriented toward this type of response but also, due to tradition, or some other extenuating circumstance, need to respond in a strong, overt way. For example, when he preaches on "Surmount Your Hangups and Give Your Life to God," he culminates that service by singing one verse of a closing hymn. While the organist plays the remaining verses, he encourages those who need this kind of help to come quietly and kneel in prayer at the chancel.

EXAMPLE 9: BURNING PLEDGES

A pastor in Louisiana preached one morning on stewardship with special emphasis on the importance of tithing. He encouraged the congregation to pledge all they could, do it for the best motives, and in the highest secrecy as a symbolic gesture of their private devotion to God. He then closed the service by having the worshipers fill out their pledge cards. After everyone had a chance to make their private commitment he then had the worshipers file by the chancel by rows and drop their cards into a neatly burning fire! He then said, "This is your pledge before God. Let's see if you really mean it!"

EXAMPLE 10: INCORPORATE MEMBERS

On those isolated occasions when the subject for the morning is church membership, churchmanship, or a number of kindred subjects, a highly appropriate change of pace from the standard M.O. could be an invitation to come forward and join the church, or perhaps in the case of existing membership, to rededicate one's life to the task of being the church in the world.

EXAMPLE 11: AMEN!

I once heard a preacher in Chicago present an excellent sermon on the general theme, "God is here, your life can never be the same again, what will you do about this confrontation?" When the final question was brought to a great climax the preacher simply said, "Amen," and walked out of the pulpit. I don't think the preacher could get away with that every Sunday, but for that special subject decisiveness was thrown right in the congregation's lap: What *are* you going to do about it?

EXAMPLE 12: INTERCESSION

A pastor once preached on intercessory prayer and closed the worship experience with the following invitation. He invited anyone who wished to come to the chancel as a stand-in (representation, not substitution) for prayer for someone they knew who needed Christ, was facing doubt, needed healing, had loved one in danger, etc. He then prayed an intercessory prayer for those known only to God who were represented that morning. It was an excellent decisive concept following such a sermon on prayer.

EXAMPLE 13: FAMILY UNITY

On Mother's Day a pastor in Tennessee invited all family units to the chancel following the sermon. He had preached on the importance of the family and how much each family needs each other and God. He dismissed the service by asking each family to join hands and participate with him in a prayer for their home.

The illustrations are as endless as your combination of imagination and inspiration. Whether useful or not useful, stimulating or depressing, these examples remind us of two very important steps the proclaimers must take if they are to be decisive in their work: (1) they will find for themselves a regular workhorse which will enable them to comfortably extend a meaningful invitation to response, and (2) they can watch with sensitivity for occasions where other models will grant both diversity and invitational opportunity to the auditing congregation. Whether you plan for a response or not, the congregation will make a response. Why not make it intentional and invitational?

10. HELP BEYOND OURSELVES

If I had to execute this critical and awesome task, the task of being a decisive and invitational minister of our Lord Jesus Christ, and do it on my own, I would quit today! I absolutely depend on help beyond myself and believe with all my heart that help is provided, available, and intensely practical. I thank God for this provision, the presence and power of the Holy Spirit, and so press on in this challenging work.

The great British Methodist preacher, William E. Sangster once said, "The doctrine of the Holy Spirit is Methodism's great buried treasure. Some day she will dig it up again, and once again she will shake the world!" That statement had to be both a fervent prayer as well as a shining hope. If you and I together ever make a difference, again it will be because we have rediscovered that great buried treasure. For what we need in our life of decisive ministry is this power made available by a God who called us and therefore by a God who will provide for our obedience.

I speak of the able and practical assistance of the Holy Spirit in John Wesley's terms, a second work of grace, a Divine Enabler. Though I deeply respect and appreciate much that was preserved and accomplished by the floodtide of the so-called "Charismatic Movement," in the mid- and late 1970s and early '80s, I speak not of a *gift* but of a *Giver*. I speak of the need and availability of help beyond ourselves in the New Testament sense of the term. I want help in my frightening and delightful task that is applicable for what I face. I do not want to dip into the trunk of religious phenomenology and come up with a badge that makes me acceptable to a specific religious peer group.

We should make a clear distinction between two important and closely related New Testament Greek words; grace (*charis*) and gifts (*charismata*). *Grace* is a free gift according to Ephesians 2:8,9: "For *grace* you have been saved because through faith; and this is not your own doing, it is the *gift* of God—not of works, lest any person should boast." *Charismata*, on the other hand, is a special gift God gives us to do a special job according to 1 Corinthians 12).

I no longer play golf. Several years ago I came to the conclusion that if I wanted to be frustrated I would go to a committee meeting down at the church. Prior to this time, however, I played regularly. On one occasion I was on the course with three other clergy. We were preparing to tee off on

the seventeenth hole at Ironwood Golf Course in Gainesville, Florida. I
was the first up, and as we were coming down the stretch I wanted to win
badly. I especially wanted to beat my close friend who trailed me by only
one stroke. The seventeenth green at Ironwood is a dogleg to the left
extending about 300 yards. I teed up and put the ball safely on the fairway
about a nine iron from the green. My friend, in order to offset this good
placement, decided to gamble. In the curve of the dogleg was a rather
prohibitive cypress swamp. My friend decided to use a three wood and
attempt to loft the ball over that swamp and place it directly on the green.
He teed up, hit the ball flat and sailed it right into the middle of that
cypress head just skimming along the water. I stood there thinking,
"There really is a God!" Then, suddenly, we heard a dull thump as the ball
struck some ancient cypress tree deep in that swamp and then stood
there aghast as the ball lofted up over the creek that separated the swamp
from the bend in the dogleg and settle comfortably about ten yards ahead
of my shot!

The two of us stood there, backing up players forever, and had our
biggest theological argument. I insisted that what happened to him was
charis, the undeserved grace of God. He insisted that it clearly wasn't.
What happened to him was *charismata*, God's special gift which enabled
him to do what he had to do. I was right, but he won the game!

In this chapter I focus on *charismata*. Not *charis*, for that is what
enables us to know Christ in our lives. Not *charismatic* because that
could be but a preoccupation with one of the gifts of the Spirit. I speak of
charismata, a marvelous New Testament word containing so much hope
for us. Put another way, the Charismatic looks for *a* gift while *charismata*
is an openness to *whatever* gift is needed to accomplish a given task. God
provides this virtual storehouse of enablement for faithful disciples. God
gives us real help beyond ourselves! This help is not doing for us what we
are perfectly capable of doing for ourselves, it is enablement to go beyond
what we can do. It is not the kind of grace, as someone has said, that takes
us up to our extremities but is the kind of grace that takes us beyond our
abilities.

If you wish to study this concept biblically, then engage in a more
thorough study of John 14:15-16. This passage reads, "If you love me you
will keep my commandments. And I will pray the Father and he will give
you another Counselor, to be with you for ever." That is, people who really
love are obedient, and in whatever obedience God asks of us he will give
us help beyond ourselves to get it done! This theological understanding is
found in the word *comforter*.

Until I made a more thorough study of this passage I never really appreciated the word *comforter*. To me it always generated thoughts of a "rock-a-bye-baby" theology. The word conjured up a concept of faith that bespoke comfort only and, having done so, left me not fully appreciating the deeper theological and practical ramifications.

Reading in the works of William Barclay really helped me here. Barclay helped me understand that the original Greek word, *paraklatos*, was translated "comforter" in the 1611 King James Version because, for that day, it was an adequate and meaningful translation. In 1611 the closest Anglo-Saxon word to a literal translation of the paraklatos was the Latin word *fortis*. Fortis literally meant to send someone in to help dispirited soldiers. It was, for instance, a word used in the siege of a castle. If the castle were about to fall, and the defending soldiers had given their very best, and the cavalry all of a sudden appeared on the horizon, this was refortifying and as such, a great comfort.

In the Greek, the word *paraklatos* actually means "one who is called in." This is why, for instance, Moffatt translates it as "helper," and other translators use similar words. The Greeks used the terms in reference to a witness called into a law court on a person's behalf, or one who is called in to advise a person in difficult decisions, or reinforcements in an armed struggle, or a morale booster in a drooping cause. The Greek army, for instance, called their reserve troops the paracletes. This meant the same as it does in modern warfare. It means that if the army in the field has done its best but is being steadily driven back, then reserves are brought forward to help out. The Paraclete, therefore, is an enabler beyond one's own gifts, graces, and grit. God steps into the fray when we have given our best but now need more than we possess within ourselves. What a comfort!

In essence, Jesus was saying to his disciples that even though his work was finished, and he was getting ready to leave, he still sent them out on a tough task, a very difficult engagement. Disciples then and now are to be involved decisively in bringing the Good News of God to the needs and anguish of people. You are to be an evangelist! This means you are commissioned to provoke confrontation, practice reconciliation, demonstrate redemption, be a peacemaker, troublemaker, and surgeon of the soul and society. If you think this job is bigger than you are, then you are right! You will need help beyond yourself and Jesus provides that help for you! He gives us a Presence that can take us beyond our extremities. "Take comfort and, if you truly love me, be obedient!"

Now, the practicalities of this great promise are recorded for us in Galatians 5:22 and 1 Corinthians 12:4-11. Galatians tells us of the "fruit" which the Paraclete can make healthier and 1 Corinthians tells us of the "gifts" which the Paraclete, the Spirit, can make stronger and more effective.

God calls us to be more loving, patient, kind, faithful, self-controlled, or any or all the fruit of the Spirit. God's promise incorporates the assurance that if we try our best to be like Christians are supposed to be, when we have done our best and are about to blow it, God will step in and help us with love or patience beyond ourselves.

The promise also holds that if we will go out and attempt to do the job to which we are called, God will place upon our limbs the enablement for this job. Depending on the job, God may give us the gift of wisdom, faith, the ability to heal, or the ability to do some miraculous thing, or a special voice to impart a truth that may strengthen someone else or, as a prayer language, at least strengthen us for the task!

Help beyond ourselves! How comforting! How enabling! How practical! This help beyond ourselves is expressed through a passage from Charles Raven's work, *Experience and Interpretation*.

> On the occasions when (a preacher) is 'at his best,' when his thoughts flow clearly and his words give eloquent expression to his message, when a close relationship is established between him and his hearers and they respond quickly and sympathetically to his slightest change of mood, he is apt to discover that though they go away pleased and interested nothing of any importance has in fact occurred. He and they have had a pleasant meeting, and that is all. But on occasions when he has seemed quite unable to express the experience that haunts him, when words are hesitant and commonplace, when speech is an effort, almost an agony, and he comes away feeling exhausted and ashamed, having 'let down God and failed to help (people)' he gets evidence that in fact a real experience has been made possible, that though his phrases are not remembered nor his arguments discussed, his hearers have found a communion not with him but with God.

The passage helped me recall that God calls me to give my best and then realize that my best is not enough, that God needs me to allow myself to become a channel for God's grace and presence. And that, when I have given my best, it is God's entrance as Paraclete that makes the work of the Spirit truly happen. I try never to ask, "Was I good or bad? Did I struggle or fly?" I try only to ask, "Was I obedient? Did I give my best? Can I now count on help *beyond* myself?"

Wesley called this experience a second work of grace. I adapt this expression to call it "knowledgeable commitment." One finds, upon reflection, that all commitments have two dimensions: initial and knowledgeable. Marriage, for instance, has the initial commitment which is made up of love, emotional response, and a naive wonder about what we are entering. But there comes a time in that relationship where we begin to understand that marriage is a growing up, maturing process. At that point, we have either to get out of it or make a *knowledgeable commitment*. At that point, we might "pray" for the "spirit of marriage"!

A young man in our church joined the Marines on impulse. His initial response was one of pride, excitement, and glory. Boot camp quickly informed him of the other dimension to all commitments. Knowledgeable commitment set in and he went away somewhere to "pray" for "the spirit of a Marine."

This analogy applies to faith commitment. There is the initial commitment, one made of response to love, forgiveness, and other attractive ingredients known or unknown to us. Then, there inevitably follows the time when the only thing that will sustain us is knowledgeable commitment. We now have the knowledge to know the depth and responsibility of this commitment. Consequently, if we are to stay, serve, or survive, we draw aside by ourselves and pray for the Spirit of God to take over our lives!

When the spirit of marriage, Marines, or faith is invited to enter our lives, we then find help beyond ourselves. A retired pastor from St. Petersburg, Florida once told me, "The disciples had the greatest three-year seminary any group of ministers ever had. They actually walked with Christ for those years and learned directly from him. "But," he cautioned, "Always remember. They did not shake the world until they received the Holy Spirit in a practical and healthy walk."

By receiving the Holy Spirit, by accepting this Enabler, this Paraclete, we take a second step. It is a deliberate step predicated on knowledge of the task and a willingness to accept the help available to be about the task. Yes, this is when our ministry may begin to shake our immediate world. We now have more than "us." We have God's very own Spirit of ministry. We see it precisely as is stated in Acts 1:9, "You shall receive *power* when you receive the Holy Spirit." We will often feel impotent, discouraged, and totally ineffective. But, God promises us that when we give our best, and do all we can do in a particular task, God the comforter will step in and take it further because, God works beyond our extremity.

Remember that "God has not called me to be successful but to be faithful." God calls me to surrender my life to Christ (an initial surrender requiring only response to love and acceptance) and then make a knowledgeable commitment by accepting, truly accepting by faith, the Spirit that supplies and enables me in my discipleship.

The only way to conclude this chapter, for a book that gives help toward fulfilling our ministry of invitation, is to extend an invitation. How does one actually receive the Holy Spirit in his/her life?

I once heard E. Stanley Jones recommend these four important steps in making this particular knowledgeable commitment.

1. Believe God wants to give you help in your discipleship, in your ministry.

2. Be sure it is *the Holy Spirit* you want! Do not look for a gift, but be open to the Giver. Do not seek a product, but surrender to the Producer. Be very sure it is the Holy Spirit you want and not something you can control, or that will give you acceptance within some religious peer group. Turn your life over to a Presence that can control you!

3. Be willing to pay the price! That price is laying all you have in God's hands. The price is *unconditional* surrender.

4. Bring the matter to a crisis. As you would realize in a marriage or at boot camp in the Marines, you can see what is ahead, and what you need to meet it, but you cannot learn enough, acquire enough, believe enough about it to make it happen. You must *submit* yourself! You must get on your knees, at least in your heart, and say, "Here am I, Lord, send me, fill me, use me." In faith, bring the matter to a crisis, move ahead, and make the surrender unconditionally.

Then be an evangelist! Go out and invite others to also bring their worship experience to a crisis, to say "Yes," "No," or "Wait" concerning the proclamation of the hour. Invite them to join with you in the marvelous experience of Christian ministry in a lost and needy world!